ROLL OF THUNDER, HEAR MY CRY

Mildred Taylor

AUTHORED by Carrie-Anne Dedeo
UPDATED AND REVISED by Rachel Nolan

COVER DESIGN by Table XI Partners LLC
COVER PHOTO by Olivia Verma and © 2005 GradeSaver, LLC

BOOK DESIGN by Table XI Partners LLC

Copyright © 2011 GradeSaver LLC

All rights reserved. No part of this publication may be reproduced, transmitted, or distributed in any form or by any means, electronic or mechanical, including photocopy, recording, any file sharing system, or any information storage and retrieval system, without the prior written permission of GradeSaver LLC.

Published by GradeSaver LLC, www.gradesaver.com

First published in the United States of America by GradeSaver LLC. 2006

GRADESAVER, the GradeSaver logo and the phrase "Getting you the grade since 1999" are registered trademarks of GradeSaver, LLC

ISBN 978-1-60259-049-6

Printed in the United States of America

For other products and additional information please visit
http://www.gradesaver.com

Table of Contents

Table of Contents

Biography of Taylor, Mildred (1943-)

Mildred Taylor was born in Jackson, Mississippi on September 13, 1943, to Wilbert Lee and Deletha Marie (Davis) Taylor. She later said she "was born in a segregated city in a segregated state in a segregated America." The Taylors had lived in Missisissippi since the time of slavery. However, only three weeks after their daughter's birth, the Taylor family moved to Toledo, Ohio. Mildred Taylor remained there until graduating from the University of Toledo in 1965.

Several outbreaks of racially-motivated violence had occurred in the Jackson area around September 1943, and Taylor's father decided to seek a new life for his family in the North. He chose Toledo because he already had a large network of friends and relatives there. Even after their move, the Taylor family took long car trips to the South, and Mildred's experience of this environment provided the settings for her future novels.

In the South that the Taylors visited, segregation was a tangible reality. However, for Taylor, the South of racism and segregation was also a "South of family and community." Familial strength is an important theme in Taylor's books, and stories about her family (aunts, uncles, and great-grandparents), as told by her father, were a staple of Taylor's childhood. Taylor calls these stories "a different history from the one I learned in school" and credits her father's storytelling with her decision to become a writer.

Taylor's father attempted to instill in Mildred and her sister, Wilma, an awareness of their past and future. When the family moved into a newly integrated Toledo neighborhood, ten-year-old Mildred was the only black child in her class at school and realized that her actions might be judged as representative of her race. She was shocked by the "lackluster" histories of African-Americans which she found in her history textbooks. When she shared her knowledge of black history with the class, however, the students and teacher thought that she was inventing stories.

Despite the fact that she lived in the North, when a black student was chosen as the homecoming queen at Taylor's school during her freshman year (1957) many white students reacted with anger and even violence, reminding Taylor that racism was far from dead.

Taylor attended college at the University of Toledo and spent much of her free time writing, a process she found difficult, but at which she was determined to succeed. At first, she patterned her writing after Charles Dickens and Jane Austen but she soon found emulating their literary styles to be unnatural. Taylor's first novel, written at the age of nineteen, was entitled Dark People, Dark World. Told in the first person, this story of a blind white man in Chicago's black ghetto was never published, though one publisher expressed interest in a shortened version.

After college, Taylor applied for and was selected to join the Peace Corps in Ethiopia. Her father was both proud of his daughter and worried about her being so far away for so long. After graduating with a degree in education from the University of Toledo, Taylor accepted the Peace Corps assignment and taught history in Ethiopia.

Upon returning to the United States in 1967, Taylor worked as a Peace Corps recruiter from 1967-1968 and as a Peace Corps instructor in Maine in 1968. In the fall of 1968, Taylor matriculated at the University of Colorado's Graduate School of Journalism. There, during the era of Black Power, she joined the Black Student Alliance and was instrumental in the creation of a black studies program at the university. After receiving her Master of Journalism, Taylor worked for the Black Education Program as a study skills director.

During her involvement with the BSA, Taylor studied black culture, black history, and black politics. She was approached by Life magazine to write an article about the BSA, but the magazine disagreed with Taylor's portrayal of the organization and never published the article. Disappointed, Taylor returned briefly to Ethiopia.

Taylor moved to Los Angeles after returning to the United States and worked at a number of temporary jobs. She refused a job at CBS as she grew more and more interested in writing. In August 1972, she married Errol Zea-Daly. The two divorced in 1975 and have one daughter.

Taylor's first big break came when she won a contest sponsored by the Council on Interracial Books for Children. Her winning piece, Song of the Trees (1975), was a revision of an old manuscipt based on a family story about trees cut down by money-hungry white men. Taylor had originally planned to tell the story from the point of view of her grandmother, but found it to be more successful when told from the perspective of eight-year-old Cassie Logan.

Roll of Thunder, Hear My Cry was Taylor's second book about the Logan family. Published in 1976, it won the Newbery Award, which recognizes excellence in books written for children. The book was dedicated to Taylor's father, who the characters of Stacey and David were based on. A television miniseries adaptation starring Morgan Freeman aired on ABC TV in 1978.

Another Logan family book, Let the Circle Be Unbroken (1981), continues the story of the family's struggle during the Great Depression. The fourth Logan family book, The Road to Memphis (1990), revisits Cassie as a high school senior attending school in Jackson, Mississippi. Both books met with critical acclaim. A related book, Mississippi Bridge (1990), is narrated by Jeremy Simms, a white character from Taylor's earlier books about the Logans. Taylor's latest Logan book, The Well: David's Story (1995) depicts ten-year-old David Logan (Cassie's father).

Taylor wrote two other books, The Friendship and The Gold Cadillac, both published in 1987, which also address the theme of racism. The former narrates the course of a relationship between a white man and a black man in 1930s Mississippi that eventually becomes violent, and the latter is based on the trips Taylor took to the South as a child with her family.

Currently living in Colorado, Taylor received the Jason Award for The Well: David's Story in 1997. She is also a multiple recipient of the Boston Globe Horn Book Award, the Jane Addams Book Award, the Coretta Scott King Award, and the Christopher Award.

About Roll of Thunder, Hear My Cry

Roll of Thunder, Hear My Cry is a product of three different eras of black history. The injustices portrayed in the book have their roots in the era of slavery which lasted until the Civil War and which, shamefully, continues to influence racial conduct in America in the 1930s and today. The book itself takes place in 1933, during the Great Depression. Roll of Thunder, Hear My Cry represents a South in which racist sentiments had tangible effects in the form of segregation, lynch mobs, and unfair distribution of resources. Mildred Taylor wrote Roll of Thunder, Hear My Cry in the 1970s, at the height of the Black Power movement and at the beginning of an increasing presence of African-American history in education.

Mildred Taylor's own ancestors were slaves in the state of Mississippi, as were the ancestors of the novel's protagonist, ten-year-old Cassie Logan. Her grandmother, Big Ma, tells stories about Cassie's grandfather, Paul Edward, who was born a slave two years before the Civil War. Taylor herself heard stories from parents and relatives about the former-slaves in her family and used those stories as inspiration for her novel.

Slavery began in the United States in the 1600s and quickly became widespread, especially in the South. It developed into an economic necessity for an economy based on plantation crops. The invention of the cotton gin by Eli Whitney fueled the economy of Southern cotton plantations and increased the need for slave labor. Mrs. Logan's lesson to her seventh grade class about the economic impacts of slavery stresses that this arrangement benefited the national economy as a whole, since Northern factories depended on Southern raw goods, at the expense of unpaid, forced labor. Slaves also cleared the wilderness of the expanding country and built canals, railroads, and roads.

Mr. Morrison's mention of his parents being "breed stock" illustrates the result of such an economy on its least powerful members. As Mama explains to Cassie, selected slaves were often forced to "breed" to create a stronger new generation of workers. By 1860, there were four million slaves in the United States. Slaves had no right to marry, to own property, to testify in court, or earn their freedom.

Though slave emancipation came along with the Northern victory in the Civil War, the realities of Reconstruction created an environment in which racist hatreds and discriminatory laws continued. Laws requiring literacy, land ownership, or a grandfather who had voted as a prerequisite for voting kept many blacks disenfranchised until as late as the Civil Rights Movement of the 1960s. Jim Crow laws, which developed primarily in the 1890s, created a segregated society in which blacks and whites attended different schools, rode in different train cars, and drank at different drinking fountains. This state of affairs remained the norm until the pivotal court case, Brown v. Board of Education, when "separate but equal" was deemed fundamentally unequal. Black schools, like Great Faith Elementary and Secondary, were generally far inferior and more poorly funded than their white counterparts.

Discrimination and segregation continued throughout the 1930s, during which Roll of Thunder, Hear My Cry takes place. The Great Depression began in 1929, when the stock market crashed. A forty-percent drop in the price of farm products and resulting foreclosures on many farms in the early 1920s contributed to the crash. Between 1929 and 1933, the years in which the novel is set, the price of farm goods fell a further fifty percent. In 1933, the unemployment rate was twenty-five percent (thirteen million people). Mr.Morrison, having lost his job on the railroad, faced the far from uncommon troubles of the unemploted. Because of the lack of jobs, those who had jobs were often forced to accept undesirable working conditions in order to remain employed. In the novel, Papa works a less than ideal job, laboring months of the year away from his family on the railroad in Lousiana.

The Civil Rights Movement of the 1960s and the resulting Civil Rights Act of 1964 and Voting Rights Act of 1965, signed by President Lyndon B. Johnson, ended de jure segregation in America. Still, de facto segregation and discrimination remained. Race riots in Harlem in 1964 and the Watts district of Los Angeles in 1965 resulted from the continued, often systematic discrimination by whites against blacks and the resulting inequality in living conditions. The assassination of Martin Luther King, Jr., a leader of the Civil Rights movement, by James Earl Ray in 1968 demonstrated to many blacks the continued danger that they faced based on the color of their skin.

Roll of Thunder, Hear My Cry is Taylor's second book about the Logan family. Her first book, The Story of the Trees, was published by Dial in 1975 and earned her first prize (African-American category) from the Council on Interracial Books for children, an outstanding book of the year citation from the New York Times, and a Jane Addams Honor citation. Therefore, when Taylor published Roll of Thunder, Hear My Cry in 1976, she was doing so in a safe literary environment which had embraced her previous depiction of the Logans' encounters with racism in 1930s Mississippi. The Story of the Trees had been praised by the New York Times Book Review for "dramatic tension and virtuoso characterization" and by the Bulletin of the Center for Children's Books as "fairly brisk, verging on poetic."

Even more than its predecessor, Roll of Thunder, Hear My Cry met with critical praise. It was awarded the prestigious Newbery Medal for children's literature, cementing Taylor's reputation as an author. Other awards included a notable book citation from the American Library Association, a National Book Award (finalist), an honor book citation from the Boston Globe-Horn Book, and a Jane Addams Honor citation.

Taylor has spoken explicitly about her intentions in writing Roll of Thunder, Hear My Cry, saying that she hopes that it "will one day be instrumental in teaching children of all colors the tremendous influence Cassie's generation had in bringing about the Civil Rights movement of the fifties and sixties." She credits the inspiration for the book to her father, a member of that very generation. She says,

"Without his teachings, without his words, my words would not have been."

Character List

Cassie Logan

Cassie is the first-person narrator of the novel. At ten years old, she is the second oldest and the only female child in her family. Cassie is intelligent, outspoken, and self-confident, even when those qualities threaten to get her in trouble for speaking her mind in a white-dominated world. Over the course of the novel, Cassie directly experiences racism and learns the real dangers of being black in the South in the 1930s. At the beginning of the novel, Cassie is proud of herself and her race but unaware of the possible consequences of this pride. She is witness to the violence and injustice of the South as she becomes aware of lynchings, of the curtailment of her father and mother's freedom, and of the severe punishments meted out to blacks accused of wrongdoing. Cassie grows up over the course of the year, learns some sad truths, and experiences the strength and love of her family.

Stacey Logan

At twelve years old Stacey is on the brink of adulthood. As the oldest child, he bosses his brothers and sister around and is the leader of their small group. He is old enough to disobey his parents but not old enough to fully appreciate the consequences of doing so. His dawning awareness of racism leads him to make difficult choices, like pushing away his white friend Jeremy. In the end, he proves his bravery and loyalty by risking danger and by attempting to help his estranged friend, TJ. He also uses his ingenuity to protest against injustice. For example, it is his idea to build a trench in the rain-filled road to stall the white children's school bus.

Christopher-John Logan

At age seven, Christoper-John is a short, chubby boy who is the quietest Logan sibling. He is always cheerful but frequently reminds the other children that they are breaking their parents' rules. Despite his misgivings, he usually ends up following his other siblings to avoid being left behind.

Clayton Chester "Little Man" Logan

Little Man, age six, is a smart boy with a highly developed sense of right and wrong. Able to read before he started school, he partakes in his older siblings' adventures and in doing so learns a great deal about the racist South.

David "Papa" Logan

A tall, handsome man, Papa is Big Ma's second youngest son. He works from the end of planting until Christmas on the railroad in order to pay for his land. He was raised on the same farm on which his family now lives. Ready to stand up for himself and his family, he does what he "gotta do" to survive and respect himself. He risks his life to institute a boycott against the Wallaces, store owners who burned a black man to death. His leg is broken and he is shot at in retribution for the boycott. He also comes close to losing his land when the bank, influenced by Mr. Granger, calls in the note on it in. He is willing to use his shotgun to protect TJ but ultimately uses his ingenuity to stop the lynch mob and save TJ's life, even though his strategy loses him a quarter of his own cotton. Papa believes that his family and the land must be protected at all costs.

Mary "Mama" Logan

A thirty-three year old woman from the Delta, Mama went to high school in Jackson and was sent to the Crandon Teacher School by her tenant-farmer father. Her father died during her final year in teacher school, and she married Papa when she was nineteen. She has taught at the Great Faith school for fourteen years, and has four children of her own. Her strong pride in her race and her sense of justice lead her to paste over the inside covers of the schoolbooks, where the "very poor" condition of the book is listed next to the race of the black students. This outspokenness results in her being fired by the white school board. Though she tries to keep stories of the violence and injustice around them from her children, she ultimately cannot shield them from the truth.

Caroline "Big Ma" Logan

Papa's mother is a woman in her sixties. She holds the deed to the Logan land, which was bought by her late husband, Paul Edward. She married him when she was eighteen, and they raised their six children, only two of whom survived, on the four hundred acres of land that he bought between 1887 and 1918. Big Ma is the voice of history in the book and tells stories about the past to Cassie. Her love of the land leads her to sign it over to her two sons to protect it from Harlan Granger. She has medical knowledge and is often called upon to tend those injured by white violence, including the Berrys. She is very religious and is a source of comfort to Cassie who shares a room and bed with her.

Hammer Logan

Hammer is Big Ma's only living son other than Papa. He lives in the North and drives a Packard like Mr. Granger does. He visits the Logans during the Christmas season and brings gifts. He has a strong temper and wants to attack Charlie Simms after his bad treatment of Cassie. Ultimately, he quells his temper when he must and sells his Packard in order to protect the land, bringing the money to his brother by hand and leaving before his presence can fuel more tensions.

Mr. Morrison

Mr. Morrison is an extremely big and strong older man whom Papa brings home from the railroad. Mr. Morrison got in a fight with some white men and was fired from the railroad. He helps to protect the Logans, watching outside their house at night, and stays on with the family even after he injured the Wallaces when they attacked Papa. His own family was brutally murdered by a lynch mob during

Reconstruction and he says that the Logans are like family to him.

TJ Avery

An emaciated-looking, thirteen-year-old boy, TJ is foolish but provides a source of information about racial incidents for the Logan children. He is repeating the seventh grade, cheats on tests, gets Mama fired, and hangs out at the Wallace store which ultimately loses him Stacey's friendship. His "friendship" with the older, white Simms brothers leads him to commit a crime and nearly causes him to be lynched. He is the catalyst for an eruption of racial tension and at the end will most likely be sent to a chain gang for a murder that the Simmses committed.

Claude Avery

TJ's younger brother does not say much but is also a friend to the Logans. He is more afraid of TJ than of their mother and generally does what his brother tells him to do. He is beaten by the mob when they come for his brother.

Mr. Avery

TJ and Claude's father is a sharecropper on Harlan Granger's land. He participates in the boycott of the Wallace store but backs out when Granger threatens to kick him off the land. He is small and sickly and can't control TJ. He too is treated violently when the mob comes for his son.

Mrs. Avery

TJ and Claude's mother has little control over her sons. When she tries to protect her son from the mob, she is thrown back against her house.

Jeremy Simms

Jeremy is a towheaded white boy, probably about eleven, who wants to be friends with Stacey. While the other white children ride the bus, he always walks to school. He is whipped by his father for associating with the Logans. He dislikes his older brothers and sleeps in a treehouse to get away from his family.

Lillian Jean Simms

Aged twelve or thirteen, Lillian Jean is Jeremy's older sister. She has long blond hair, which Cassie makes use of when fighting her. She is shrill and bossy. Her father forces Cassie to call her "Miz Lillian Jean" and apologize after bumping into her in Strawberry.

RW and Melvin Simms

Jeremy and Lillian Jean's older brothers are about eighteen or nineteen years old. They pretend to be friends with TJ, who steals things for them, and for whom they buy things. When he helps them break into the Barnett Mercantile to steal a gun, they kill Mr. Barnett and injure Mrs. Barnett. Afterward, they beat TJ and lead the mob that breaks into the Avery house and tries to hang him.

Charlie Simms

The father of the Simms family is a "mean-looking man, red in the face and bearded." He twists Cassie's arm behind her back and forces her to apologize to "Miz Lillian Jean" when she bumps into her on the sidewalk in Strawberry. He is not involved in the attack on the Avery house, but is woken up by Jeremy who smells smoke from the tree-house. Cassie and Little Man see him working side-by-side with Mr. Lanier to put out the fire at the end of the novel.

Harlan Granger

Granger owns a ten-square-mile plantation which is worked by sharecropping families. The Logans' land had belonged to the Granger family before it was sold to a Northerner during Reconstruction, and Mr. Granger's desire to get it back from the Logans leads him to threaten Big Ma and to use his authority in town to pressure the bank to call in the note on the mortgage. He, Kaleb Wallace, and a third man, representing the school board, fire Mama for teaching history that isn't in the books and for defacing the school's books. When the boycott on the Wallace store begins, he recognizes the possibility of financial loss to himself because he owns the land that the store is located on. He decides to take sixty rather than fifty percent of his sharecroppers' cotton and threatens to kick out those who continue the boycott. On the night of the attack on the Averys, Granger lets Jamison tell the crowd that he doesn't want a hanging on his land but does little to stop the mob until the fire threatens to engulf the forest and his crops. Only then does he force the mob to fight the fire rather than to hang TJ.

Kaleb, Thurston, and Dewberry Wallace

These three white brothers own the Wallace store, the only store in town. They sell alcohol illegally and host a room where black teenagers dance. The store is on Granger property, making it profitable for Harlan Granger as well as the Wallaces. The Wallaces burn the three black Berry men, killing one and severely injuring the other two, after drunk white men accuse John Henry Berry of flirting with a white woman. When the Logans arrange a boycott on their store, the Wallaces attempt to ambush Papa on the way back from the market in Vicksburg. Mr. Morrison beats up two of the Wallaces badly, nearly breaking Dewberry's back and laying up Thurston for a few weeks as well. The Logans cannot press charges against the Wallaces because to do so might result in Mr. Morrison getting put on the chain gang or worse. The Wallaces are involved on the attack on TJ and the other Averys, and Kaleb leads the cry to hang TJ.

Mr. Wade Jamison

A lawyer whose family was originally from Vicksburg, he inherited land that had once belonged to the Grangers from his father and sold it to Paul Edward Logan in

1918. Cassie likes him for always calling her mother "ma'am." He offers to back the credit of those who boycott the Wallace store and shop in Vicksburg, and he stands opposed to those who want to hang TJ, arguing with them and even blocking them from driving away by putting his car in the middle of the road.

Mr. Montier

Mr. Montier is a plantation owner. The children of his sharecroppers attend the Great Faith school, though many choose not to make the three-and-a-half-hour walk after they finish fourth grade in Smellings Creek, which is nearer to his estate. He too raises the percentage of cotton his sharecroppers owe him and threaten to evict them if they continue the boycott.

Mr. Harrison

Mr. Harrison is another plantation owner whose sharecroppers' children attend Great Faith. He is a "decent man" and doesn't raise his percentage of cotton or threaten to evict his sharecroppers because of the boycott.

Jim Lee Barnett

The owner of the Mercantile in Strawberry cheats his black customer, Sam Tatum, and when Tatum accuses him of lying, "night men" tar and feather Tatum. When TJ tries to buy goods for his mother at the store, Barnett stops serving him and ignores him for an hour while waiting on white customers. When Cassie politely tries to remind him that they are waiting, he calls her a "little nigger," and throws her out of his store. When the Simms brothers and TJ break into his store, he comes down to investigate and RW hits him over the head with the flat part of an axe. He dies the next morning.

Mrs. Barnett

Mrs. Barnett is the wife of the owner of the Mercantile. Hearing her husband scuffling with the Simmses, she goes down to investigate. RW pushes her back against the stove and she is knocked out. She thinks that the three intruders are all black because RW and Melvin wear stocking caps over their faces.

Little Willie Wiggins

A seventh grader at Great Faith Elementary, Little Willie tells Cassie, Christopher-John, and Little Man how Stacey was whipped by Mrs. Logan when he was caught with TJ's cheating notes. He also tells them that TJ told Kaleb Wallace about Mama pasting over the book covers in order to get her fired.

Mr. Wiggins

Little Willie's father owns forty acres of land six miles away from the Logan farm.

Moe Turner

Another seventh grader at Great Faith, Moe stands at the crossroads on the day Stacey is whipped for having TJ's cheating notes and points Stacey towards the Wallace store when he wants to find TJ. He lives on the Montier plantation and must walk three and a half hours each way to and from school.

Gracey Pearson, Alma Scott, and Mary Lou Wellever

These snobby girls in Cassie's class are all friends and don't want her to sit with them. Mary Lou is the principal's daughter and the only girl wearing a new dress on the first day of school.

Miss Daisy Crocker

Her fifth grade teacher has great contempt for Cassie Logan. She whips both Cassie and Little Man when they object to the used "very poor" books that have been given to black students on the first day of school.

Mr. Wellever

The principal of Great Faith Elementary and Secondary School is powerless to do anything but stand and watch as Harlan Granger, Kaleb Wallace, and another school board member fire Mama.

Mr. Silas Lanier

Another black tenant-farmer, Mr. Silas Lanier got Big Ma to tend to the Berrys the night that they were burnt. He pulls out of the boycott of the Wallace store after Mr. Granger's threats. Cassie and Little Man see him working side-by-side with Mr. Simms to put out the fire at the end of the novel.

Mrs. Lanier

The children learn the details of the Berry family's burning by overhearing Big Ma talk with Mrs. Lanier and Mrs. Avery after church.

John Henry, Beacon, and Samuel Berry

These are members of a family that lives by Smellings Creek. John Henry, who owns a Model T, is accused by some white men of flirting with a white woman while getting gas with his brother Beacon in Strawberry. That night, they are burned alive along with their uncle Samuel by a group of white men led by the Wallaces. John Henry dies and Mama takes the children to visit Samuel Berry and his wife as punishment for going to the Wallace store. Mr. Berry is burned beyond recognition and cannot even speak.

Sam Tatum

A black man who lives on Jackson Road near Strawberry, he calls Mr. Barnett a liar after he denies cheating him. In retribution for this accusation, the white "night men" tar and feather Mr. Tatum.

Mr. Grimes

Mr. Grimes drives the Jefferson Davis school bus and takes sadistic pleasure in forcing black students off the road. The Logans seek revenge on him by digging a trench in the muddy, rainy road.

Sheriff

The sheriff does whatever Mr. Granger says he should and turns a blind eye to violence against blacks. He makes no move to stop lynch mobs.

Major Themes

The importance of family

There is one lesson Cassie need not learn throughout Roll of Thunder, Hear My Cry because it is already second nature to her: that there is nothing more important than family. Cassie's shock when Jeremy says that he does not like his older brothers demonstrates her firm belief that family is more important than anything else. From Big Ma's stories about her husband and sons to Mr. Morrison's willingness to risk his life to protect the Logans, it is clear that love of and devotion to family is the motivation that drives the majority of the characters in this novel to act as they do. Those who behave like TJ and abandon their families ties are lost, but those like Papa, who is willing to risk even death to protect his family, triumph.

Land as a symbol of independence

Repeated again and again throughout the book is a refrain spoken by Big Mama, Mama, and Papa: "we won't lose the land." In a culture where the memory of slavery is still strong, land is a symbol of independence and autonomy. Because they own land, the Logans can afford to shop in Vicksburg and are not beholden to the whims of landlords as sharecroppers are. Unlike Mr. Granger who sees the land as a symbol of his family's "rightful" domination over blacks, for the Logans, the land is intrinsically linked to family. Cassie says that it doesn't matter whose name the deed is in because it will always be "Logan land." It is only when she realizes the seriousness of the threats to her family and their land that she cries "for...the land" at the end of the book.

Weather as echo of human emotions

Weather is more than a meteorological phenomena. As the words to Mr. Morrison's song suggest, weather is a sentient entity capable of hearing his cry and empathizing. The dust, rain, and mud emphasize the white degradation of the black school children, and the physical barrier posed by walking to school in the rain echo the barriers erected to the black children's education by the school board. The climax of the book occurs simultaneously with a massive thunder storm, and the approaching storm cannot be separated from the approaching violence. Ultimately, however, this weather is empathetic. The rain which comes and puts out the fire helps to bring about an end to both the physical and emotional storm.

Hope in the face of destruction

Throughout the book, situations occur from which no escape seems possible and in which the loss of land or life, seems inevitable. When faced with the worst, however, Taylor's characters ultimately pull through their troubles. Uncle Hammer, when called upon to pay the bank note, does not lose his temper or threaten violence but instead willingly sells his beloved Packard car. Most illustrative of this theme is the scene in which black and white men and women work side by side to put out the fire. These are the same people who had been previously threatened each others' lives and livelihood. When faced with a common threat, they cease to see the differences of race and identity between them.

Passage of time as a cycle

Roll of Thunder, Hear my Cry fills the course of a year, beginning with the cotton harvest and ending with another approaching harvest. The time periods in the book are delineated more often by cycles of weather than by real time: dusty, hot fall; rainy, muddy winter; beautiful, green spring; and carefree summer. Big Ma always reassures Little Man that the rains will end and the sun will shine again. This theme of hope and change is reflected in Cassie's final thoughts in the book. She and her brother will resume their normal life, but TJ will not. This emphasis on time as a cycle is usually a source of hope because it offers a promise that whatever hardship is occurring will eventually cease. At the same time, it is a source of constant fear in a racist and often violent society. The tensions that grew and erupted with the beating and arrest of TJ will calm down, but will eventually grow and erupt again.

Coming of age through experience and pain

Roll of Thunder, Hear My Cry is a coming of age story for Cassie, as she realizes the extent of racism in the South over the course of her tenth year. At the same time, Cassie learns the importance of love, family, and self-respect. For Cassie, it is through personal humiliation during an incident in Strawberry that she must learn that life is not fair; through the pain of watching TJ's destruction she learns that even the smallest offense by even the youngest black person can bring about irrevocable punishment; from her parents worries about losing the land she learns that nothing is truly secure. Stacey, like Cassie, must learn from similar experiences. But for both, these realizations are significant only in that they spark newly mature reactions of responsibility, love, and caring. To respond in a more foolish manner, as TJ did, would be to seek to be treated as a man while acting like a boy and therefore be unfairly meted the punishment of a man.

Friendship as risk

It is no accident that the Logan childrens' closest friends are each other, for they share the same values and know that they can trust one other. Papa tells Stacey that friendships between blacks and whites are a risk, as TJ's friendship with RW and Melvin later demonstrates. At the same time, Jeremy's persistence in seeking TJ's friendship shows him to be a true friend, and the impossibility of their friendship is a sad circumstance of their environment. Despite his anger at TJ for his previous wrongs, Stacey shows himself to be a true friend when he is most needed, risking his own safety to try to save TJ.

Doing what you "gotta do"

Papa talks to his children about the fig tree which has just as much right to grow in the ground as the other, bigger trees, and just keeps on growing, "doing what it's gotta do." For Papa, this philosophy does not excuse excessive cruelty or violence but rather speaks to the necessity of sacrifice. Papa sacrifices his own cotton and puts himself in danger when he starts the fire to save TJ's life. Sacrifices sometimes include doing distasteful things to ensure survival, for example, when Big Ma must force Cassie call Lillian Jean "Miz." But according to Papa's philosophy, self-respect, not necessity, inspires doing what you gotta do. Papa urges his children to be true to themselves, and to do both what they must do to survive and to respect themselves at the same time.

Greed as a cause of hatred

The lesson that Mama is in the middle of teaching when the school board fires her is a particularly apt one. She is not just teaching of the cruelties of slavery but also of the economic benefits that led whites to enslave blacks in the first place. Harlan Granger and Kaleb Wallace, who fire Mama, both make a great deal of money from white subjugation of blacks--Granger from sharecroppers and Wallace from customers without cash who have no choice but to shop at his store. The hatred felt and acted upon by Granger, Wallace, and others feeds this greed. By ensuring through acts of violence that they can pressure and control blacks, they also ensure the continuance of an economic system that benefits them. Granger's desire to buy the Logan land is intertwined and inseperable from his hatred of blacks. Even his actions in calling to mob off to go put out the fire are inspired by his greed. Papa recognizes and capitalizes upon this greed when he comes up with the strategy of setting the fire in the first place.

Independence and self-respect

Mary and David Logan instill self-respect and independence in their children. It is a testament to Cassie's self-respect that she is utterly shocked by Mr. Barnett's treatment of her in his store. The same self-assurance explain's Little Man's reaction to the derogatory statements in his textbook. In the course of the story, the children must learn to balance survival with self-respect. Hammer, with his short temper, has difficulty doing so. TJ, because he has so little self-regard, ends up ruined. For all of the characters, self-respect is born of independence, of choosing freely and accepting the responsibility for their choices. Examples of this responsibility include when when Mr. Morrison leaves it up to Stacey to confess going to the Wallace store or, more seriously, when Papa weighs the risks and still chooses to go to Vicksburg.

Glossary of Terms

attorney
lawyer

bank
slope of land adjoining a body of water

carpetbagger
derogatory term for northerners who moved to the South after the Civil War to make a profit from Reconstruction

chignon
a roll of hair worn at the back of the neck

churn
stir, as in making butter

clapboard
a structure made of slats of varying thicknesses

emaciated
extremely thin

ember
the coal or ash of a dying fire

glade
open space in a forest

gravelly
low and scratchy

gully
a deep ditch or channel

indignant
righteously angered

lynching
a hanging executed by a mob, usually racially motivated

mercantile
country store

molding dish
apparatus that shapes the finished butter

ransack
plunder, pillage

share-cropping
a tenant farmer who gives his landlord a share of his crops rather than rent; a common system in the South post-slavery

snaggle-toothed
full of teeth that are broken or misaligned

switch
whip

welts
marks left over from a beating

Yankee
Civil War term for a person from the North

Short Summary

Nine-year-old Cassie Logan heads to the first day of school with her brothers, twelve-year-old Stacey, seven-year-old Christopher-John, and six-year-old Little Man. It is October, 1933, and they are the children of an African-American couple living in rural Mississippi. The family owns four hundred acres of land, half of which is mortgaged, and Papa must work half the year on the railroad far away to pay for it. Mr. Granger, whose family owned the land during slavery times, wants to buy it back and constantly threatens to coerce them into selling it to him.

On the way to school, TJ Avery and his younger brother, Claude, tell the Logans that the Berry family were burned by the white Wallace brothers. A white boy, Jeremy Simms, joins them for part of the walk. He goes to Jefferson Davis County School while the Logans attend Great Faith Elementary. At school, Cassie and Little Man get in trouble with the teacher, Miss Crocker, by protesting that their used textbooks list the condition "very poor" next to their race. Mama, who is a seventh-grade teacher, pastes paper over the inside covers of her students' books to hide this information.

Papa returns unexpectedly from the railroad with a very big, strong man named Mr. Morrison, who got in a fight with some white men and lost his job on the railroad. He will be staying with the Logans.

In October, the children must walk to school in the rain and mud and are splashed by the vindictive driver of the white school's bus. (The black school cannot afford a bus because the county does not give it enough money.) One day, after being forced off the road into a muddy ditch, Stacey leads his siblings in digging a trench across the road at lunchtime to make it look like the road has washed out. After school, they watch from the forest as the bus drives into the ditch, breaking its axle, flooding its engine, and leaving the white students without a bus for two weeks.

Later, the children hear that the "night men" are out. Cassie sees cars approach the house in the middle of the night and then turn around. Later, TJ tells the Logan kids that these men tarred and feathered a black man, Sam Tatum, for accusing Jim Lee Barnett, who owns the Mercantile in the neighboring town of Strawberry, of cheating him.

Stacey takes the blame when he is caught with TJ's cheat-notes during a test. He follows TJ to the Wallace's store, where he has been forbidden to go, and punches him. Mr. Morrison catches him and brings him home. Stacey confesses to Mama, who punishes the four children for going to the store by taking them to see Mr. Berry, who is burned so badly that he is not recognizable and can no longer speak. Mama begins to arrange a boycott of the Wallace and Barnett stores.

Big Ma takes Stacey, Cassie, and TJ to the market in Strawberry. While Big Ma talks to Mr. Jamison, a friendly white attorney, TJ admires a pistol in the main store. When Mr. Barnett waits on white customers while ignoring TJ, Cassie tries to remind him of their presence. He calls her a "little nigger," then throws her out of the store for arguing with him. In the street, Cassie bumps into Jeremy's sister, Lillian Jean, and is forced by Mr. Simms to say, "I'm sorry, Miz Lillian Jean," as Big Ma looks on.

Uncle Hammer comes to visit for Christmas, hears this story, and is only prevented from going after Mr. Simms by Mr. Morrison. Mama explains to Cassie that Big Ma had no choice but accede to Mr. Simms' wishes. Uncle Hammer drives the family around in his new Packard and also gives Stacey a new coat. TJ makes fun of him because it is so big on him until Stacey gives it to TJ to borrow until he grows into it. Uncle Hammer makes him give it to TJ permanently for being irresponsible enough to let TJ take it from him in the first place. On Christmas, Mr. Morrison tells the story of how, when he was six years old, his entire family was killed when an angry white mob attacked his house, where two young men accused of molesting a white women were hidden.

Big Ma puts the land in Hammer and Papa's names to protect it. Mr. Jamison agrees to provide credit for the families who have agreed to have Papa shop for them in Vicksburg rather than patronize the Wallaces' store. Mr. Granger, who owns the land upon which Wallace store sits, threatens Uncle Hammer and Papa with the loss of their land.

Cassie pretends to be friends with Lillian Jean, acting subservient, calling her Miss, and carrying her books for her. One day she takes her into the woods and fights with her, pulling her hair until she apologizes for the incident in Strawberry. Cassie threatens to tell the secrets that Lillian Jean has shared with her if she says anything to her father. Mama fails TJ on a test for cheating. In retribution, he mentions to the Wallaces that she has covered the inside of the books. Kaleb Wallace, Harlan Granger, and another man from the school board come to Mama's class when she is teaching a lesson about the injustices of slavery and fire her.

Stacey stops being friends with TJ, and TJ starts hanging around with RW and Melvin Simms, who are older and are white. Mr. Avery, Mr. Lanier, and several other people stop buying goods in Vicksburg when Mr. Granger and Mr. Montier raise the percentages of cotton they want from their sharecroppers and threaten to kick anyone who continues the boycott off their land. On the way back from a trip to Vicksburg to buy goods for the few families still participating in the boycott, Papa, Mr. Morrison, and Stacey must stop when the back wheels fall off their wagon. As they fix them, the Wallace truck stops behind them and someone shoots at Papa, grazing his temple. The horse tries to run away, and the wheel of the wagon rolls over Papa's leg, breaking it. Mr. Morrison fights off the Wallaces, badly injuring them.

With his new injury, Papa can't go back to work on the railroad, but it looks like the family might scrape by until the bank calls in the note on their mortgage. Uncle Hammer sells his Packard to pay for it. He brings the money to his brother's family on the week of the revival, a religious and social event, but must leave quickly so as not to incite further tensions. TJ shows up at the revival with RW and Melvin, who he says will buy him the pistol at the Barnett store. When Stacey and everyone else ignore him and enter the church, TJ is upset but finally leaves with the Simms brothers.

That night, thunder rolls and Mr. Morrison keeps watch outside the house. TJ taps on the door in the middle of the night and tells Cassie and Stacey that he broke into the Barnett Mercantile with RW and Melvin to steal the gun. When Mr. Barnett came down to investigate the noises, RW and Melvin, who were disguised with stockings over their faces, hit him with the flat side of an axe. When his wife came down, they threw her against a stove, knocking her out. TJ threatened to tell the police, so the Simms boys beat him up badly. He asks Stacey to help him get home, and all four Logan children end up walking TJ back to his house in the middle of the night.

The Logan children watch from the woods as the Wallaces, Simms brothers, and other whites break their way into the Avery house and drag out its inhabitants, beating them. Many of them call for hanging TJ, Mr. Morrison, and even Papa. Mr. Jamison arrives and tries to stop them. Stacey sends the other children home to tell the adults what is happening.

After hearing the story from Cassie, Papa sets off with his shotgun and Mr. Morrison. Soon, Mama notices smoke coming up off the cotton, which is burning. She and Big Ma go out to fight the fire, which is heading towards the woods. Before dawn, Jeremy Simms comes to the house and says that all the white men (whom Cassie and her brothers saw at the Averys' house) have gone to fight the fire. He has also seen Papa and Stacey, who are all right. Just then, it begins to rain heavily, which puts the fire out.

Cassie and Little Man rush to the cotton fields where they see white and black men and women putting out the rest of the blaze. Mama and Big Ma take them and Stacey home. There, Stacey tells Cassie that Mr. Jamison tried to stop the hanging, but Mr. Granger would not cooperate until he smelled smoke and sent the men to fight the fire. That is when Mr. Morrison (strangely, not Papa) went to get Stacey in the woods. Cassie realizes that the lightening didn't start the fire, but rather, Papa started it. Papa and Mr. Morrison arrive home and Papa tells Stacey and Cassie that TJ is with the sheriff and will probably be put on the chain gang where he might die. Stacey bursts into tears and runs off. Papa follows his son after putting Cassie to bed. In bed, Cassie cries for TJ and the land.

Summary and Analysis of Chapters 1-2

Chapter One Summary:

Cassie Logan and her three brothers (Stacey, Christopher-John, and Little Man) walk down a dusty road in rural Mississippi on their way to the first day of school in the fall of 1933. Stacey, aged twelve, is grouchy because he will be in the class taught by their mother. Christopher-John, aged seven, is a cheerful boy who keeps to himself. Cassie is annoyed that they must go to school on a "bright August-like October morning" and is even more annoyed that they must wear their Sunday clothes and shoes.

Little Man is six years old. It is his first day of school ever, and he walks very slowly and carefully to avoid getting the dust from the road on his shoes or corduroys. Cassie tells him that he will make them late to school, and she drags her feet in the dust until Stacey yells at her to stop because they promised their mother that they would arrive neat and clean.

As they walk, the children pass an old oak tree that marks the boundary between their family's four hundred acres of land and the forest. The forest and the land beyond is part of Harlan Granger's ten-square-mile plantation. The Logans' land had once belonged to the Grangers. Cassie's grandfather bought the family's first two hundred acres in 1887, and after he paid off the mortgage on that land bought two hundred more in 1918.

The Logans still have a mortgage on the second two hundred acres of land and have to pay taxes on all four hundred acres. In 1930, the price of cotton dropped, and the profit from their cotton crop could not pay the Logans' bills, so Cassie's Papa left to look for work. Every year, Papa works in Louisiana on a railroad, and is away from home from spring until the next winter.

Cassie remembers Papa telling her that the land is important because as long as she lives she will never have to live on anybody's place but her own. Cassie knows that the land belongs not only to her Papa but also to her brothers, their grandmother, their mother, and their uncle. Papa describes it as "Logan land." While Papa is away, Mama teaches school and Big Ma works in the fields.

Halfway to school, an "emaciated-looking" barefoot boy named TJ and his brother Claude emerge from the trees and walk with the Logan children. TJ failed Mrs. Logan's class the previous year and will be in it again with Stacey. He tells Stacey that Mr. Berry and his two nephews were burned by some white men the previous night. Stacey says that Mr. Lanier had fetched Big Ma to help nurse Mr. Berry the night before. TJ knows about the burning because Mrs. Logan had stopped by to talk to his mother about it before school earlier that morning.

TJ is angry at Cassie for telling her mother who told his mother about him going up to the Wallace store to dance. He only escaped being whipped by telling his mother that he only went up there to follow Claude, who wanted to buy candy. Cassie knows that Claude was willing to take TJ's punishment because he is more scared of his brother than of his mother.

The children have to jump out of the way as a school bus rushes by and covers them with dust. Stacey explains to Little Man, who is furious, that the bus is only for white children and that they don't have a bus. A blond white boy named Jeremy runs out of the forest and starts walking with the Logans. He tells Stacey that his school has been going since the end of August. Cassie recalls that Jeremy has always walked with them to the crossroads in the morning and met them there after school. Other kids at his school pick on him because of this and he sometimes has red welts on his arm as punishment for associating with them, but he continues to meet them.

At the crossroads, some other white children rush past and Jeremy's older sister, Lillian Jean, yells at him to come with them. Cassie looks at the white children's building, Jefferson Davis County School, and notices that it has two school buses, a sports field, and the Mississippi flag with the emblem of the Confederacy on it. The black children turn east to head to their school.

They go to Great Faith Elementary and Secondary School, "consisting of four weather-beaten wooden houses on stilts of brick, 320 students, seven teachers, a principal, and caretaker, and the caretaker's cow." Most of Cassie's classmates are children whose families sharecrop on three nearby plantations. They start school late because their families need them to pick cotton until October.

Cassie walks slowly over to the building that houses the first four grades. Mary Lou Wellever, the principal's daughter says hi, and Cassie notices that she is wearing a new dress. Cassie looks at the other children wearing their Sunday clothes and knows that after today, they will come to school barefoot again until the roads freeze. She also sees Stacey's friend Moe Turner, who walks to school for three and a half hours from the Montier plantation.

Inside the school, Cassie sits with Gracey Pearson and Alma Scott, who say they would rather have Mary Lou sit with them. When the teacher, Miss Daisy Crocker, tells everyone to sit down, Mary Lou looks angrily at Cassie. The first and second grade teacher, Miss Davis, is in Jackson for a few days, so Miss Crocker temporarily teaches both classes.

Miss Crocker announces that they will all have books this year. Cassie has never had one of her own before and is excited until she notices that they are old and worn. She sees how excited Little Man is to get a first grade reader because he cannot see the cover. Cassie picks up her book and begins to read it until she hears Miss Crocker yelling at Clayton Chester (Little Man) because he has asked for a book that is not dirty.

Little Man takes the book back to his desk, but when he opens it, sees something inside it that makes him throw it on the floor and stomp on it. Cassie looks inside her book and sees columns listing the book's condition and the race of the student for every year from 1922-1933. This is the first year that the book's condition is listed as "very poor" and the first time that the race of the student is listed as "nigra" instead of "white." As Miss Crocker is about to take the switch to Little Man, Cassie explains that her brother can already read and shows the teacher why he was angry. Miss Crocker tells Cassie that the books says "nigra" because that's what she is and orders her to sit down. Cassie tells Miss Crocker she doesn't want her book either. Miss Crocker takes the switch to both Little Man and Cassie.

After class, Cassie is determined to tell Mama the story before Miss Crocker does, but accidentally bumps into the principal, Mr. Wellever, and receives a long lecture from him on watching where she is going. When she gets to her mother's classroom, she sees Miss Crocker showing her the book that Little Man broke. Miss Crocker cannot understand why the children got so upset about what was written in the inside cover. Though Mama says that Miss Crocker had the right to punish them for disobeying, she clearly doesn't agree with her. Mama trims brown paper to the size of the page and glues it over the inside covers of her children's books. Miss Crocker is shocked that she would "damage" county property, but Mama says she is going to do it to all the seventh graders' books the next day. Cassie can tell that her mother understands, and sneaks away.

Analysis:

This chapter provides an introduction to the social and historical structure of black life in the South in the 1930s. The educational system functions as a microcosm in which the reader can see the greater inequalities in society reflected in the differences in schooling available to black and white children. The black children must walk for an hour (or in Moe's case, three and a half hours) to get to school, while the white students have school buses that will drive them directly there. The physical ease with which the white children attend school reflects their greater access to education. Cassie personifies one of the two buses as "our own tormenter." The bus is a tormenter not only because it sprays them with dirt as it passes but also because in doing so, the bus illustrates society's that they are somehow inferior to, or dirtier than, the white children.

Similarly, the physical differences in the structures and appearance of the schools demonstrates the cultural and physical divide which separates black and white society in the 1930s South. The white children's school is named after Jefferson Davis, the president of the Confederacy. Cassie notes that the Mississippi flag "waving red, white, and blue with the emblem of the Confederacy emblazoned in its upper left-hand corner" flies over the white school. This flag is a symbol of segregation and oppression. Flying over the white school, the flag's presence illustrates that the "ideals" of the Confederacy, including oppression of blacks, still exist many years after the Civil War.

Cassie notes that the Mississippi flag flies above the American flag. The positioning of the flags illustrates the domination of racist Jim Crow ideology over the more inclusive American ideal of equality. "Jeremy and his sister and brothers" can "hurr[y] toward those transposed flags" because they represent a system which will allow them power and success, but the black children must turn away and head in the opposite direction.

The incident with the schoolbooks demonstrates the ability of the children themselves to recognize the system of symbolic as well as actual oppression. Little Man lives up to his name in that he is far more perceptive than the teacher, Miss Crocker, in reading the deeper meaning behind the columns in the front cover or his book. The equation in Cassie's book of "very poor" and "nigra" illustrates not only the county's contempt for black children's educational needs but also reminds the reader that characters like TJ and Claude, who have no shoes, or like the Logans, whose father must work away from home for months to afford taxes and a mortgage, are poor as a result of discrimination.

Cassie recognizes the power of language more clearly than Miss Crocker does. Miss Crocker attempts to push her students into action by making them respond in unison to her. Cassie's refusal to respond to Miss Crocker's request that she "share, share, share" comes in part because she recognizes the futility in saying something that you don't mean. "I never did approve of group responses," she thinks. Cassie also fails to respond because she is thinking of something more meaningful: the burning of the Berrys.

Furthermore, Cassie recognizes the danger inherent in the abuse of language. She says "S-see what they called us," when showing Miss Crocker the book, assuming that the teacher will think the labeling as wrong as she does. Miss Crocker, who later urges Mrs. Logan to make the children accept the way things are, cannot contemplate any means of resistance because she accepts the labels given to her by the whites in power. By accepting the racial title written in the book, she also accepts a type of subordination.

Chapter Two Summary:

Big Ma watches as Cassie balances halfway up a pole in the cotton field. She, Christopher-John, and Little Man are all picking the last of the cotton at the tops of the plants. (Stacey is too big to climb the poles now.) Big Ma tells Mama that they have picked enough for the day.

From the top of her pole, Cassie sees Papa and another man coming down the road. The children rush over to hug them, and he says they're getting too big to call his "babies" anymore. The other man with them is Mr. Morrison, who is very tall. He has burn scars on his face and neck, deep wrinkles, some gray in his hair, and "clear and penetrating" eyes. Mama wants to know if something is wrong, but Papa avoids the question.

Mr. Morrison and the family walk into Mama and Papa's room, which doubles as a living room. Mr. Morrison looks around the room, the walls of which are covered with pictures of various family members, before sitting down in Grandpa Logan's rocking chair. Big Ma asks her son how long he will be home, and he tells her until Sunday evening. It is already Saturday. The children want him to stay longer, but he says that if he does, he will lose his job.

Papa says that he came home to bring Mr. Morrison, who is going to work in the house as a hired hand for room and board and a few dollars in the winter. He used to work on the railroad but cannot get work anymore. Mr. Morrison, whose voice is "like the roll of low thunder" says he got fired from his job because some white men started a fight with him and he beat them up. They didn't get fired.

That evening, as they milk the cows, Cassie asks Stacey if Papa brought Mr. Morrison home because of the burnings. Stacey tells her not to worry about it. Cassie says she just wishes she knew more. Christopher-John, close to tears, says that he wishes that Papa could stay at home.

The next day, at church, Mrs. Lanier tells Big Ma that John Henry Berry died the night before. The deacons announce it as well, and the people pray for his soul and for his brother and uncle's recovery. After church, Mr. Lanier says that John Henry had a nice place up by Smellings Creek with a wife and six children and that "they" have been after him since he came back from the war. Big Ma says he was just in the wrong place at the wrong time.

Mrs. Lanier says that Henrietta Toggins, who is related to the Berrys, was with them in John Henry's Model T when it happened. They had stopped for gas and some drunk white men came by and said: "That's the nigger Sallie Ann said was flirtin' with her." Henrietta made John Henry and his brother Beacon get in the car and drive off without filling up on gas. After they dropped her off at home, the three white men caught up with them and kept hitting the back of the car. Knowing he didn't have enough gas to get home, John Henry stopped at his uncle's. The white men dragged John Henry and Beacon out of the house and when their uncle tried to stop them, lit all three of them on fire.

TJ's father says that he heard that a boy was lynched in Crosston a few days ago. Mr. Lanier says that the worst thing is that no one can do anything about it. The sheriff called Henrietta a liar when she went to him, and now the white men who did it are bragging about the lynching, saying "they'd do it again if some other uppity nigger get out of line." Papa says that his family doesn't shop at the Wallace store. The room goes silent. After the Laniers and Averys leave, Papa tells the children that Mama has heard about other older kids going to the store to dance, buy bootleg liquor, and smoke. He says he does not want his children going there and says he'll "wear [them] out" if they go there. The children agree not to go, knowing that Papa swings a mean switch.

Analysis:

The power of language is once again prevalent in this chapter. The use of derogatory, racist terms and the act of racist hate-crimes are part of a continuum of power. In their society, the white men face no reprimand for calling Henry John derogatory names. This too-permissive atmosphere implicitly condones the growth of their hatred into physical action.

For this black community, language is both powerful, and, in their own mouths powerless. All the white men need to do to "justify" their attack on the Berrys is say that Henry John was flirting with a white woman. This second-hand hearsay is the only reason that they appear to have for attacking the Berrys. Similarly, their later bragging and threats operate just as strongly as physical threats. At the same time, black language does not have the same power in white society. Henrietta's testimony is powerless to make the sheriff investigate. Truth, therefore, is an essentially meaningless concept in this society, where the power of language is determined by race rather than by validity.

The allusion to the novel's title functions as a means of foreshadowing Mr. Morrison's significance in the novel. His voice, Cassie notices, is like "the roll of low thunder." Understanding that Mr. Morrison may be in danger, the reader can equate the threat represented by the sound of thunder with the threat to Mr. Morrison. His presence in the story marks the first entrance of an outsider into the safety of "Logan land" and suggests that, like thunder before lightening, Mr. Morrison's presence will herald dangerous changes.

Mr. Morrison's physical appearance is symbolic of his place in society. The scar on his face and deep lines show he has been literally, as well as economically, hurt by a white society that will dismiss a black man defending himself but will not fire his two white aggressors. Mr. Morrison's penetrating eyes demonstrate his spirit of resistance and his ability to see to the truth. His immediate explanation to Mrs. Logan of why he lost his job shows how highly he values the truth.

Summary and Analysis of Chapters 3-4

Chapter Three Summary:

In October, the weather turns to heavy rain, and the Logan children are soaked walking to school. The driver of the white children's school bus enjoys splashing them with mud when he drives by. This particularly upsets Little Man, who can't understand why the black children don't have a school bus of their own.

One day, the weather starts out looking beautiful but quickly turns into a thunderstorm as the Logan and Avery children walk to school. A water-filled gully separates the road and the forest bank, which is too slick with mud in some places to climb. At first they wait on the bank where the gully is narrow and easily passable, but they figure that they have left too early to meet the school bus.

At TJ's suggestion, they set off down the road rather than wait in the rain, and five minutes later the bus passes, veering close to them and forcing them to jump in the slimy, muddy gully to avoid being hit. A furious Little Man tries to throw mud at the schoolbus from which the white children yell "Nigger!" and "Mud eater!" When Jeremy tries to join them walking to school, Stacey ignores him.

Stacey makes Little Man, Christopher-John, and Cassie promise to meet him in the school toolshed at lunch. They take buckets and shovels and return to the spot where they were forced off the road. There, they dig a ditch across the area that fills with gully water and makes it look as if the road washed out from the rain.

After school, they rush back to the spot that they had worked on. As a result of hard rain during the afternoon, their "yard-wide ditch" has become a "twelve foot lake." They hide in the forest bank and watch as the Jefferson Davis schoobus approaches. Thinking that it is a puddle, the driver drives the bus straight into the hole, breaking the axle and waterlogging the engine. The white kids fall in the muddy ditch on their way out of the bus and must walk home in the rain. The bus driver tells them it will probably be two weeks before the bus can be towed and fixed.

That evening, Mama tells Big Ma that she heard Mr. Granger tell Ted Grimes, the bus driver, that they will have to wait until the rain stops to move the bus. She and Big Ma both admit that they are happy that it happened. The children are secretly proud of their revenge and cannot help laughing until Mama separates them to do their homework in different parts of the house.

Just then, Mr. Avery appears at their door and announces that "They's ridin' t'night." Mama sends the children straight to bed, but Cassie sneaks around the outside of the house into the boys' room. They hear that the "devilish night men" have been "set off." Cassie worries that the men are coming after them because of what they did to the bus, and Stacey feels as if it were his fault because it was his idea to dig the ditch.

Cassie sneaks back into her room and pretends to be asleep as Big Ma pulls a shotgun out from under the bed and sits at the window. Later in the night, she wakes up and Big Ma is gone. She goes out on the porch to revisit the boys' room and then hears something, but it is only Jason, the hound dog.

Just then, headlights from a series of cars approach the house. Jason hides, but Cassie sits frozen as two men get out of the cars and stare at the house. Then, one man waves the others away and the cars all turn around and drive off. When they are gone, Jason begins barking and Cassie sees Mr. Morrison standing at the side of the house, holding a shotgun. She goes inside and goes back to bed but cannot fall asleep until dawn.

Analysis:

Once again, thunder plays a symbolic role in Cassie's world. On the morning of the incident with the schoolbus, the children set off with sun behind the clouds, only to have the weather change quickly. "Soon the thunder rolled across the sky, and the rain fell like hail upon our bent heads." The seemingly unpredictable changes in the weather mirror the children's seeming luck in escaping the bus. The hope for sunny weather is dashed when the thunder storm begins just as the children's hopes of escaping the schoolbus where the gully is smallest are dashed when they end up jumping into the muddy gully.

Earlier in the chapter, Big Ma has assured Little Man that the sun will shine again. Her words are an intentional metaphor, reminding the child not to lose hope. Though the children temporarily lose hope after being forced into the gully, they triumph over the bus in the end, not only forcing the white children to walk home that day but also for two weeks thereafter.

Cars, too, function as symbols of power and of self-determination. Mr. Granger's is the first car that the reader sees in this chapter. For him, the car is a possession which, like his land, demonstrates that he is rich. But the car is also a means of showing that Mr. Granger has more control over his transportation, and thus his life, than the Logan children or parents have over theirs.

In this chapter, cars are solely a white possession. White children ride the schoolbus, while black children walk. White landowners (Mr. Granger) drive cars while black landowners (Mama) walk. Even more explicitly, cars are a symbol of whites' power over blacks' lives. Cassie does not need to see the occupants of the train of cars in the night to know that they are white and threatening. Whites' responses to blacks' possession of cars demonstrates that they are symbols of power. The Berry's were burned by angry white men after driving around town in their car, a transgression of race lines.

Big Ma's suggestion that Little Man might someday have a car, then, may remind the reader that even if that day comes, Little Man may have something to fear from white men. On the other hand, it may illustrate her hopes for a world in which her grandchildren can drive cars safely and freely.

In this society, blacks who outwardly hold power seem dangerous to whites. That is why even children like Cassie and her brothers must exercise their power subversively and secretly. Even children as young as Cassie and Stacey realize that if someone had seen them, the mob could have come after them.

The train of cars that turns around in the Logans' driveway demonstrates that children are not exempt from the danger that faces adult blacks. Notably, Cassie witnessses the cars' arrival alone. Even the dog, Jason, leaves her and hides. Despite the fact that mama tries to shield her children from the truth by putting them to bed early, Cassie's realization of the danger that her family could face is one step on her way to growing up.

Chapter Four Summary:

One Sunday, Cassie helps make butter and hears Mama and Big Ma talk about how she and the children have been acting strangely for several weeks. She cannot tell her mother what is wrong because she and her little brothers promised Stacey that they would say nothing about the bus. When she breaks a dish, Mama sends her to find the boys.

In the boys' room, TJ suggests that Stacey look for the questions to the upcoming history test in his mother's room. He then tells the Logan children that the "night men" tarred and feathered Sam Tatum because he accused Mr. Barnett, who owns a store in Strawberry, of charging him for things he didn't buy. Later, when the children go outside to milk the cows, TJ returns inside to get his hat. They come in and find him looking at one of Mama's books, but he says he just wanted to learn more about the Egyptians.

On the way to school the next day, TJ offers to share his cheat sheet with Stacey, and Stacey rips it up. After school, Cassie and her younger brothers see TJ run off into the forest with three boys following him. A boy named Little Willie says that Stacey was caught with a cheat sheet which he'd grabbed from TJ in class and was whipped by his mother. Stacey and all the other children take off after TJ, and Moe Turner tells them that he went to the Wallace Store.

Stacey tries to get his siblings to go home but they follow him to the Wallace store. There, the Wallaces and the older Sims brothers make disparaging remarks about "little niggers" while older students from Great Faith dance. Stacey finds TJ and the two get in a fist-fight until Mr. Morrison arrives and breaks it up. He takes the Logan children home on his wagon and says that he won't tell their mother that they went to the store, but that it is up to them to tell their mother themselves.

When they arrive at home, they see Mr. Granger's Packard driving away from the house. He had been badgering Big Ma to sell her land to him. Cassie goes with Big Ma to a clearing of trees. This area was formed when Mr. Anderson, to whom she refused to sell the trees, chopped them down anyway before Papa came home and stopped him. She tells Cassie about marrying her husband, Paul Edward, who had been born a slave in Georgia and who was working as a carpenter in Vicksburg when she met him. They bought their first two-hundred acres of land from a Yankee named Mr. Hollenbeck who had bought it during Reconstruction from the Grangers, and the second two-hundred acres from Mr. Jamison, who was a lawyer. Harlan Granger has always wanted to buy back all the Granger land but Paul Edward wouldn't sell it. Their two daughters died as babies, their son Mitchell died in World War II, and their son Kevin drowned, and now the land is Big Mama's, Cassie's father's, and her son Hammer's. She says that she will never sell it.

Stacey confesses to his mother that he went to the Wallace store. Mama sends them to bed early and then, on Saturday, takes them to see the Berrys. Mr. Berry is burned beyond recognition and cannot speak. His wife cares for him. When they leave, Mama reminds the children that the Wallaces did that to him.

On the way home, Mama stops at different farms and talks to various families about finding another store to patronize without directly mentioning what the Wallaces have done to the Berrys. Moe's father, Mr. Turner, says that he would like to participate in a boycott, but that he has credit at the store and that driving to Vicksburg overnight, like the Logans do, would take too long. Finally, Mama convinces him to promise that if she could get him credit and buy the things he needs in Vicksburg for him, then he would be able to stop shopping at the Wallace store.

Analysis:

In this chapter, Cassie's struggle to grow up is further represented through the divisions which separate her from her mother and grandmother. Believing herself to be responsible for the "night men," she takes on adult-sized worries. Cassie's decision to hold to her promise to Stacey not to speak of the bus, even when her mother asks her what is wrong, shows the reader that the Logan children live by the same principles as their parents.

Cassie's accident, breaking the molding dish at the beginning of the chapter, illustrates her difficulties in assuming these new adult responsibilities. Cassie tries to overcome the limitations of being a child (being short) by balancing on a stool, but ultimately, she is still too small to carry these responsibilities. Her crash off the stool foreshadows her coming inability to keep her adult-size secrets to herself.

The author places this book in a long tradition of African-American literature with her reference to W.E.B. DuBois's The Negro, the book that Stacey catches TJ holding in his mother's room. DuBois believed that blacks would gain equality by proving that they could excel in education and business. TJ's attempt to use the book to cheat, then, is an ironic allusion to Mama and Big Ma's shared belief in the importance of education.

The story that Big Ma tells Cassie about her life with her husband is part of a tradition of oral narrative central to the African-American literary tradition. Paul Edward's birth, two years before slavery ended, connects the story to the tradition of slave narratives, like that of Frederick Douglass. Slave narratives usually tell a story in which a slave frees himself and gains independence through his own ingenuity. Paul Edward Logan earns his four-hundred acres of land through hard, honest work. The references to the honest white men who sold him the land (Mr. Hollenbeck, a Yankee carpet-bagger) and Mr. Jamison, who cares more about the law than farming, demonstrates that all white landowners are not racist and greedy like Mr. Granger.

Once more, land is seen as a symbol of freedom and autonomy in this chapter. Big Ma emphasizes the importance of owning the land and keeping it in the family. Unlike slavery days when families could be separated at their owner's whim, Big Ma has the power to keep her children close to her and to give her land to them. The story about Mr. Anderson, who cut down the trees that he was forbidden to buy, illustrates to the reader that neither the Logans nor their land are entirely safe.

Summary and Analysis of Chapters 5-6

Chapter Five Summary:

Before dawn on a Saturday, Cassie and Stacey depart with Big Ma in the wagon for the market in Strawberry where they will sell butter, milk, and eggs. They have never been allowed to go before, but this time TJ is going along to buy things for his mother, so Big Ma decides to take her grandchildren, too. When they get to Strawberry, Cassie is disappointed to see how small the town is. At first, she doesn't understand why Big Ma parks the wagon so far away from the entrance to the market, but Big Ma assures her that her regular customers will look for her and then tells her that the wagons near the entrance belong to white people.

After lunch, the market begins to break up, and Big Ma goes to Mr. Jamison's law office. Cassie wants to go in and talk to him, since she likes him because he always calls Big Ma "Missus," but Big Ma tells the children to wait in the wagon. After a few minutes, TJ suggests they go ahead to Barnett's Mercantile and buy the goods his mother wants, in order to save time.

At the store, TJ shows Stacey and Cassie a pearl-handled revolver in a display case, which he says he wants badly. He gives his mother's list to Mr. Barnett, but Mr. Barnett stops waiting on him to take the orders of several white customers in a row, including a young white girl. It has been almost an hour, and even though Stacey and TJ try to stop her, Cassie marches over to Mr. Barnett to remind him that he has forgotten about them. He responds angrily, telling her to get her "little black self" back to waiting and calling her a "little nigger." Cassie protests, until Stacey begins to drag her out of the store, and Mr. Barnett tells him to "make sure she don't come back till yo' mammy teach her what she is."

Outside, Stacey tells Cassie that even though she knows that Mr. Barnett is wrong, Mr. Barnett doesn't. Cassie walks down the sidewalk, thinking about Mr. Barnett's words to her, and bumps into Lillian Jean Simms, who is with Jeremy and their two younger brothers. Lillian Jean demands an apology, which Cassie reluctantly gives, and then tells her that she should walk in the street. Cassie is trying to keep from being pushed off the sidewalk by Lillian Jean when Mr. Simmons appears and twists Cassie's arm behind her back.

Mr. Simmons demands that Cassie apologize to his daughter, although Jeremy insists she already did. Cassie tries to run away and is met by Big Mama. Mr. Simms demands that Cassie say "I'm sorry, Miz Lillian Jean," and Big Mama reluctantly makes her comply. Cassie says it and runs crying into the wagon, thinking this is the cruelest day that she has ever endured.

Analysis:

Cassie's difficult path toward adulthood passes another milestone when she realizes the implications of the cliche that life is not fair. Approaching Mr. Barnett to remind him that they have been waiting, Cassie expects that he will react as she does and perceive the unfairness of her situation. When he does not, Cassie is doubly outraged, both by the injustice of his racist reaction and by this upset of her generally positive worldview.

Cassie's journey to Strawberry is a metaphor for her exposure to a wider world beyond her home. She is disappointed when she sees Strawberry because it is a small, shabby place. Racism in Strawberry is more apparent and more acceptable than it is in Cassie's smaller town. In Strawberry, Big Ma is not a supreme power but instead must bow to the will of a powerful white man, no matter how much she might disagree with him.

When Cassie cries at the end of the chapter, her tears represent her loss of innocence. Her tears do not mean that she is a child, as they did in the previous chapter when she broke the bowl, but instead show that she is being pushed away from her childhood innocence.

Chapter Six Summary:

On the way home from Strawberry, even TJ stays quiet. As they put the wagon in the barn at home, Stacey tells Cassie not to blame Big Ma because she had to act as she did. Cassie insists that Big Ma is a grownup like Mr. Simms. Their conversation stops short when they spot what appears to be Mr. Granger's Packard in their barn. They run in the house where they see their Uncle Hammer. The car belongs to him.

As Mama makes dinner, Cassie tries to tell Uncle Hammer about her day in Strawberry but Big Ma keeps interrupting her. Finally, she tells him the whole story, and Uncle Hammer wants to know if it was Charlie Simms who knocked her off the sidewalk. He jumps up, saying he has his own gun when Mama glances at her husband's shotgun, and runs outside. Mama tries to stop him, but he takes off in the Packard. Mr. Morrison jumps in with him right as he is pulling away.

Mama insists he's not going anywhere and Christopher-John says that Mr. Morrison will stop him, but Cassie and Little Man envision what he might do to Mr. Simms. Mama sends the three youngest children to bed and comes in to talk to Cassie. She says that Big Ma did what she did because she didn't want Cassie to get hurt. She tells Cassie that Mr. Simms thinks Lillian Jean is better than her because she is white, even though it's not true. He is the type of person who needs to believe whites are better than blacks to make himself feel big.

Mama tells Cassie the story of slaves who were brought over from Africa, like Big Ma's great-grandparents. White people preached that people from Africa were not human so that they could make them slaves. They taught the slaves Christianity to make them obedient but even so people like Big Ma's father Papa Luke ran away three times. After the Civil War, when Papa Luke and Big Ma's mother Mama Rachel were freed, people continued to believe that blacks were not equal to whites. People like Mr. Simms hold on to that belief to make themselves feel important. Mama says that what black people give white people is fear, not respect. Cassie may call Lillian Jean "Miss" because she has to but she calls the black girls at her church "Miss" because she respects them.

The next morning, Uncle Hammer and Mr. Morrison are both in the kitchen at breakfast, looking tired. When Cassie goes to take her bath in a tub in Mama's room, Mama tells her that Uncle Hammer will take them to church in his car. Cassie watches her mother dress and do her hair and has her fix her own hair in her "grown-up hairdo." She looks as Mama puts on her shoes, which have large holes in the soles which she has patched with cardboard.

After breakfast, Stacey tells his siblings that he asked Mama outright and she said that Mr. Morrison talked to Uncle Hammer all night and did not let him go to the Simmses. He says that Big Ma told Mama that if Mr. Morrison hadn't stopped him, Uncle Hammer would have been killed. Before they leave for church, Uncle Hammer sees Stacey's too-small raggedy coat and gives him his Christmas present early. It is a beautiful new coat. They drive to church in the Packard, which attracts a lot of attention. TJ is jealous of Stacey's new coat.

After church, they drive around town, taking the Old Soldiers road which the Rebel soldiers had marched up to save the town from Yankees. Cassie wonders if Strawberry was worth saving. When they pass the Wallace store, Uncle Hammer says he would like to burn the place because he grew up with the Berrys. Mama tells him there is another way. They reach Soldier's Bridge, which can only handle one vehicle at a time. Black people driving wagons often have to back down the bridge when a white person starts down it from the opposite side. A Model T truck has started down the bridge, but Uncle Hammer speeds the Packard across and it backs up. Its passengers, the Wallaces, all touch their hats as the car approaches, thinking it is Mr. Granger, and freeze when they see the Logan family inside. Mama says they will have to pay for this later.

Analysis:

When Cassie accuses Stacey of acting like a know-it-all since going to Louisiana with Papa the previous year (after he explains to her that maybe Big Mama didn't have a choice but to obey Mr. Simms) she demonstrates the difference in the degrees they have become aware of the realities of race in the South. The incident in Strawberry and Mama's subsequent explanation of the reasons for Big Ma's actions is the proccess by which Cassie learns a lesson that Stacey has learned a year ago.

Uncle Hammer and his Packard provides a marked parallel to Mr. Granger. On the surface level, Hammer provides a means for Cassie to see the possibilities available to black men beyond becoming farmers and workingmen like Papa and Mr.

Morrison. The Packard is a mark of status, which symbolizes that Uncle Hammer is just as good as, or even better than any white man.

Hammer also provides a contrast to Papa, a man who is normally careful and thoughtful in his reactions. Hammer's knee-jerk reaction to Cassie's experience validates its injustice, but Mama's worries about what might happen to Hammer if he confronts Mr. Simms make it clear that even a black man of high status will not receive equal protection under Southern law.

Soldier's Bridge, which the family crosses in Uncle Hammer's Packard, dates back to the Civil War and symbolizes the continued but crumbling domination of Old Southern racist attitudes that only allow one way of thought and one group, whites, to have power. That it is old and falling apart suggests that these ways too will crumble.

Summary and Analysis of Chapters 7-8

Chapter Seven Summary:

When Mama asks for Stacey's coat to shorten the sleeves, he has to admit that he has lent it to TJ until he grows into it. TJ was making fun of him, calling him preacher because of the way the coat fit. Mama wants him to get it back, but Uncle Hammer tells Stacey that if he is stupid enough to give his coat away, then TJ can keep it permanently; Stacey will not survive in the world if he lets people take things from him.

Cassie is anxious waiting for Papa to come home, but decides that she will wait to do anything to Lillian Jean until talking to him. She also wants to beat up TJ, but knows that she would be unable to. Finally, before dawn on the day before Christmas, Cassie wakes up and finds that her father is home. They spend all day cooking. That night, the adults tell stories as they sit around the fire, including a silly story about Papa and Uncle Hammer stealing watermelons.

Then, Mr. Morrison tells a story which Mama doesn't want the children to hear, but to which Papa insists they listen. One Christmas during Reconstruction, Mr. Morrison was six and lived in a shantytown with his family. Night men came in pursuit of two teenage boys accused of molesting a white woman whom had hid in his house, hoping his strong father would help save them. Mama explains that slaves were bred for strength like animals during slavery. The night men burned and killed women and children, including his two sisters, and although Mr. Morrison's parents fought hard, they both died too. Though he was only a child, Mr. Morrison makes himself remember that night.

Cassie wakes up before dawn and hears the adults talking in her parents' room about the danger of offering credit to people to shop at Vicksburg. If they use their land as collateral, they may risk losing it to Harlan Granger. On Christmas morning, the children get books (two versions of Aesop's Fables for the two younger boys, The Count of Monte Cristo for Stacey, and The Three Musketeers for Cassie). Papa tells his elder children that their books were written by Alexander Dumas who was a black man. They also get stockings of licorice, oranges, and bananas, as well as clothes from Uncle Hammer.

The Averys and their eight children come over for Christmas dinner after church. While everyone is sitting around after dinner, Jeremy Simms arrives at the door and gives the family some nuts and Stacey a flute that he carved himself. Stacey cannot understand why Jerermy brought him a gift until Papa suggests he gave Jeremy the gift of friendship in the past year. But Papa warns him that friendship between a black man and white man can never be on an equal basis and it would cost too much to find out if this friendship with Jeremy could last.

The next day, Papa whips the children for going to the Wallace store. He, Uncle Hammer, and Mr. Morrison go to Vicksburg. When they come back, Mr. Jamison visits and Big Ma signs the land over to her two sons so that it cannot be taken from them after her death and so that it will require both of their signatures to sell it. Mr. Jamison agrees to put up the credit for a group of black families to shop in Vicksburg and says that not all white Southerners feel the same way as the Grangers. Nonetheless, he reminds the Logans that the Wallace store is on Granger land and that Harland Granger lives in the past. Also, starting a boycott against the Wallace store is tantamount to saying that blacks and whites are equal by seeking to punish the Wallaces for the murder of a black man, a claim that may be dangerous in their town's current racial climate. Even if he cannot beat Granger or the Wallaces, Papa says that he wants his children to know he tried.

A few days later, after taking orders from the other families, Papa and Uncle Hammer take the wagon to Vicksburg to buy goods at the store there. The day after they get back, Mr. Granger arrives at the house. He suggests that their loan for the second two hundred acres of land might come due anytime, especially since the bank owner doesn't like people stirring up bad feelings in the community. He adds that he might have to charge his sharecroppers more than their usual portion of cotton that year, so they might not be able to pay their debts. Granger leaves after saying he plans to get the land back and that there are a lot of ways of stopping David Logan. Papa says he better make them good.

Analysis:

Christian mythology plays a strong role in this chapter, which centers around Christmas. Jeremy Simms plays the role of the Little Drummer Boy, who gives whatever he can as a gift. Cassie balks at Jeremy's gift of nuts, since her family already has so many, but Mama quiets her, knowing the importance of the very act of giving.

Giving is a significant theme both in this chapter and throughout the book. Jeremy gives unselfishly but his gift is insufficient, not because of what it is, but because it is tainted by the world in which they live. Because of their racist environment, Jeremy cannot be trusted, even though he might turn out to be a better friend than TJ. Stacey is forbidden to repay Jeremy's gift with his friendship because of the danger inherent in doing so.

Stacey's "gift" of his coat to TJ, unlike Jeremy's gift, is not unselfish but instead was given ignorantly. Uncle Hammer's decision to let TJ keep the coat emphasizes the importance of deeply considering that which you give away, whether it be clothing or friendship, because gifts have long lasting consequences.

Mr. Jamison and the Logan parents both give the gift to the community, at risk to themselves, of encouraging the boycott of the Wallace store. Their moral conviction, even in the face of danger, contrasts sharply with Mr. Granger's more selfish concerns of making money and accruing possessions. This attitude towards sacrifice is also reminiscent of Christian themes including the Wise Men's gift to the baby Jesus, the defiance of King Herod, and Jesus's final sacrifice. Mr. Morrison's parents, who died to save him, also recall this theme of sacrifice.

This chapter also highlights the power of history. Papa insists that his children hear about the night men who killed Mr. Morrison's family. Storytelling in the African-American literary tradition is more than a way to pass the time; it is also a means of testifying to and remembering the past in hopes of helping future generations.

Chapter Eight Summary:

Cassie catches up with Lillian Jean as she is walking to school and tells her that after what happened in Strawberry, she has come to see how the world actually works. She says: "I'm who I am and you're who you are," and offers to carry "Miz Lillian Jean's" books. When Lillian Jean turns toward her school at the crossroads, Jeremy tells her she didn't have to do that. Her younger brothers and TJ want to tell on her to Mama but Stacey makes them promise that they won't. Stacey also won't have anything to do with TJ's plans to cheat on the upcoming final exam.

Cassie tells the reader that on New Year's Day, after Uncle Hammer left, Papa took her to the hollow with the cut-down trees. He told her that there were some things in life that you have to do to survive and that if she makes the wrong decision about Lillian Jean, Charlie Simms will get involved and there will be trouble.

During January, Cassie calls Lillian Jean "Miz," carries her books, and listens to the secrets that she tells about the girls she is friends with. After school on the last day of exams, Cassie meets Lillian Jean on the road and tells her that she has something in the woods to show her. After walking into the woods, Cassie throws Lillian Jean's books down on the ground. When Cassie won't pick them up, Lillian Jean slaps her. After the older girl has struck her first, Cassie thinks that it is fair to fight back. Cassie has had Big Ma braid her hair flat to her head so Lillian Jean cannot pull it, but Cassie grabs onto Lillian Jean's long loose hair and twists it until she apologizes for her superior behavior and for the incident in Strawberry. Cassie lets her go saying that if she tells her father about the fight, she will tell Lillian Jean's friends all the secrets that she knows about them. Lillian Jean just cannot understand that Cassie had been fooling her and says "You was such a nice little girl..."

At school the next day, Miss Crocker makes Cassie sit in the cold back of the room, under the window, after catching her daydreaming. Cassie sees Kaleb Wallace outside. Claiming to have to go to the bathroom, she follows to watch from the top of a woodpile as Kaleb, another man, and Harlan Granger enter Mama's classroom. They say that they are representing the School Board and watch as Mama continues the history lesson she that she had been teaching about slavery. Mama talks about its cruelty and the economic benefits that the ruling class got from the free labor of others. Mr. Granger opens a student's book, with the paper pasted on the front cover, and accuses Mama of teaching things that aren't in the book, which was approved by the School Board. He fires her.

The children meet their mother after school and walk home with her. When they get home, she tells Papa, Mr. Morrison, and Big Ma that she has lost her job, and says that it is their way of getting back at the family for shopping in Vicksburg. She worries about where they will find enough money for the mortgage, and Papa says that they will manage. She goes for a walk, and Mr. Morrison offers to get a job now that Papa is back, but Papa says he will be leaving again soon. He tells Little Man that Grandpa was a tenant farmer who saved every penny to send Mama to high school in Jackson and teacher training school, and that Mama was meant to teach like "the sun is to shine."

Little Willie Wiggins tells Stacey the next day that TJ had been complaining about Mama failing him on his final exam in the Wallace store and talked about the pasted book covers in front of Kaleb Wallace. TJ has stayed home from school that day, so the Logan children follow Claude home, and Stacey accuses TJ, who tries to blame it on Little Willie. Stacey doesn't believe TJ but doesn't beat him up, saying he has something worse coming to him. At school the next week, everyone shuns TJ, who still will no take the blame. TJ tells Stacey that it doesn't matter because he has better friends now who treat him like a man and who are white.

Analysis:

The theme of friendship reappears at the end of this chapter and foreshadows disaster. Papa has warned Stacey of the danger in friendships between blacks and whites because of the inequality involved. TJ proclaims himself to be superior to the Logans, who he calls babies, because they are younger than he. The that time he spends at the Wallace store, befriending the very men who burned the Berrys, suggests that TJ is putting himself in danger.

TJ's belief that he can have white friends is contrasted with Cassie's "friendship" with Lillian Jean. Both are attempting to use these friendships to their advantage, TJ to quell the inadequacy he feels about being poor and being held back in school, and Cassie to get revenge. Unlike TJ, Cassie embarks on her "friendship" well aware that it can never be real. TJ and Lillian Jean provide interesting foils for one another in this chapter. Just as TJ boasts of his new friends, Lillian Jean does not suspect that Cassie's friendship is an act and continues to be surprised even after Cassie beats her up. Cassie care to not leave any marks on Lillian Jean's face is both pragmatic (there is no evidence against her) and metaphorical, because it shows that Cassie understands the importance of appearances in a way that Lillian Jean and TJ do not.

While Cassie is acting as Lillian Jean's "slave," TJ calls her an "Uncle Tom." In part, of course, this is an allusion to Harriet Beecher Stowe's abolitionist novel, Uncle Tom's Cabin. The word has also been transformed into a derogatory term for a black person who behaves in a sycophantic manner toward whites. This statement is in part ironic because it is TJ who is playing the Uncle Tom figure by ratting out Mrs. Logan to the Wallaces.

Summary and Analysis of Chapters 9-10

Chapter Nine Summary:

Spring comes, and classes are about to end at Great Faith at the end of March. Jeremy tells Stacey that he will miss walking with him and offers to visit his house but Stacey says that his father would not like it. Jeremy also says that TJ has been hanging around with his brothers RW and Melvin, who are eighteen and nineteen, and who make fun of TJ behind his back.

Cassie asks her mother why TJ would hang around with the Simms boys, and Mama tells her that they hang around with him to make themselves feel good and to use him. Mr. Jamison comes over and talks to Papa, who is working in the fields. At supper, Papa tells Mama that Thurston Wallace has been talking about stopping the shopping in Vicksburg but that it is not time to be scared yet.

Papa has still not left for the railroad when school ends. When Cassie begs him to stay he tells her he has to go in order to pay the taxes and mortgage. They have planted extra cotton to make up for the fact that Mama was fired. Just then, Mr. Avery arrives and says that he cannot buy things in Vicksburg anymore because Mr. Granger and Mr. Montier have asked their tenant farmers for sixty rather than fifty percent of their cotton and has threatened to kick those who shop in Vicksburg off their land. The Wallaces have threatened to get the sheriff to put those who owe debts on the chain gang. Stacey is angry after he leaves but Papa says that he does not understand the risks that Mr. Avery must face. When Cassie worries that they are giving up, Papa compares them to a little fig tree on their property. It is smaller than the other trees but keeps on doing what it has to do and does not give up.

That night, Cassie sneaks out of bed to eavesdrop on Mama and Papa talking on the porch. Papa wants to bring Stacey to Vicksburg with him so that he'll know how to handle himself, unlike TJ whose parents can no longer whip him. Seven families have decided to keep shopping in Vicksburg, so Papa, Stacey, and Mr. Morrison leave on Wednesday before dawn to do the shopping.

On Thursday, when they are supposed to get back, it begins to rain. Mama is so worried that she considers going out on the horse to look for them, but the wagon arrives. Mr. Morrison carries Papa into the house, his leg splinted with a shotgun and a rag tied around his bleeding head. Mama sends the unwilling children to bed while she prepares to set Papa's broken leg.

In the boys' room, at first Stacey will not say what happened but finally tells the other children that on the way back from Vicksburg, the back wheels fell off the wagon, probably a trick played by some boys he saw standing near it in town. Rather than unload everything, Stacey held the horse still while Mr. Morrison held up the back of the wagon and Papa attached the wheel. A truck with its lights off approached them from behind, and they didn't hear it because of the storm. It suddenly turned on its lights, Papa grabbed his shotgun, and someone in the truck shot Papa, grazing his temple. The horse reared up and the wagon rolled over Papa's leg. Papa told Stacey to hide in the gully. The men shot at and missed Mr. Morrison, who threw one of them to the ground and fought with the other two. Badly injured, the men drove off. Mr. Morrison put the wheel on and they came home.

Cassie asks who the men were, and Stacey tells her he thinks that it was the Wallaces. Christopher-John and Little Man want to know if Papa is going to die, but Stacey insists that he will be fine in the morning.

Analysis:

Previous chapters have foreshadowed retribution against the Logans for organizing the boycott of the Wallace store. Papa's comment, early in this chapter, that it is not time to be worried yet contributes to the building tension and expectation of a crisis. The attack on Papa by the Wallaces, however, does not release this tension entirely. Papa may be alive (and is clearly better off than the Wallaces' other victims, the Berrys) but there is no certainty that retribution is over. Therefore, this crisis is a minor one that increases the tension and conflict of the novel, rather than diffusing it.

This chapter illustrates that the novel is not only Cassie's coming of age story, but also Stacey's. When Mama worries about sending Stacey to Vicksburg with his father, Papa tells her that he is twelve years old, and "a boy gets as big as Stacey down here and he's near a man." The realities of life in the South mean that a young black boy cannot afford to remain a boy even at twelve. In Papa's eyes, doing so means remaining ignorant of the very real dangers of life.

Stacey's impending manhood contrasts sharply with TJ's perception of himself as a man. In the previous chapter, he told Stacey he was "fourteen, near grown." But TJ's "manhood" does not encompass the awareness of the dangers that his actions portend. He thinks that his friendship with RW and Melvin Simms makes him an adult because RW and Melvin are older. Yet Stacey already realizes he cannot be friends with Jeremy, who is his own age. The inequality inherent in TJ's relationship with the other Simms boys, who are both older and white, foreshadows a coming crisis.

Throughout the book, the author stresses the economic factors which contribute to racism. It is no accident that the history lesson that resulted in Mama getting fired was about the ways in which white Americans used black slave labor to their economic advantage. Similarly, the Wallaces' anger stems from their financial loss.

Chapter Ten Summary:

A week later, on Papa's first day out of bed, he and Mama discuss their financial situation. They have enough for the June note on the land with only a couple of dollars left, though they will have to scrimp on food. Papa plans to sell the cow and calves and maybe the old sow to pay the July and August notes, and the cotton should pay for the September note. They do not want to tell Hammer what happened and ask him for money because they are afraid that with his temper, Hammer will do something that will get him killed. Papa, however, wishes that he could react like Hammer would and whip the Wallaces. Thurston and Dewberry Wallace are still laid up from what Mr. Morrison did to them. Mr. Morrison has been looking for work with no success.

The children go with Mr. Morrison in the wagon to lend Papa's planter to Mr. Wiggins at his farm, six miles away. On the way back, Kaleb Wallace's pickup truck stops in the middle of the road, blocking their path. Kaleb threatens to gun down Mr. Morrison for hurting his brothers. Mr. Morrison calmly looks in the pickup to see if Kaleb is carrying a gun, then uses his enormous strength to move the pickup to the side of the road. As they drive away, Kaleb yells that he is going to "get" Mr. Morrison. At home, Mama worries about Mr. Morrison putting himself in danger for them but he tells her that her children are like the family he never had.

In August, the children escape the heat by sitting by the pond in the woods. Sometimes, Jeremy joins them. One day, he says that some people are glad that Papa got hurt. Mama has told Cassie that they cannot report the Wallaces to the sheriff because Mr. Morrison might get put on the chain gang for what he did to them. Jeremy also talks about TJ hanging around with his brothers. He invites the Logans to see his treehouse, since his father isn't home, but Stacey coldly refuses.

At home, Mr. Morrison returns from Strawberry with an envelope and meets Papa in the barn where he is repairing a harness. The bank has called in the note on the land, even though they have four more years left to pay. Papa is angry and wants to ride to Strawberry immediately, but Mama persuades him to wait till morning, since the bank won't even be open and he will be putting himself in danger. Big Ma worries about what they will do if Hammer cannot get the money, and Papa promises they won't lose the land.

The annual revival begins the third Sunday of August and is filled with seven days of religious services, socializing, and food. At lunch on the first day, Stacey spots Uncle Hammer walking down the road. He has sold his Packard to pay for the land and is bringing the money to Papa. Though everyone wishes he could stay longer, they think that it would be too dangerous, and Hammer leaves early Monday morning.

It seems to be about to storm on the last night of the revival, but the Logans decide to go anyway. Before the meeting, Little Willie Wiggins and Moe Turner tell Stacey that they have seen TJ with the Simms brothers. TJ and the Simmses come to middle of the gathering and TJ, dressed in trousers, a suit coat, tie, and hat, announces that they are his friends, unaware of the condescending smirks that Cassie sees on their faces. TJ says that his new friends will buy him anything he wants, including the pearl-handled pistol in Barnett's Mercantile. Stacey turns away in disgust and follows everyone into the church, leaving TJ upset that no one cares. RW says they're going to Strawberry to buy him the pistol but TJ stands, looking puzzled and undecided, before finally following them.

Analysis:

The novel continues to move towards its climax as yet another crisis occurs when the bank calls in the note. The theme of strength found in family recurs when Uncle Hammer sells his beloved car to save the land. That car had symbolized equality to Hammer, because it was the same model as Mr. Granger's. However, Hammer chooses family over the outer appearance of equality. Mr. Morrison's choice to remain with the Logans, despite the danger to himself, also emphasizes the importance of family.

The land, of course, is a symbol of the family and its strength. Possession of the land means that the Logans are not beholden to the whims of white landowners, the way sharecroppers like the Averys are. Papa's assurance to Big Ma that they'll keep the land is a recurring refrain throughout the book.

Through Stacey's relationship with Jeremy, we can see an alternate view of race relations. Jeremy's tree-house, from which he believes, or wishes, that he can see all the way to the Logans' land metaphorizes his hope for a greater connection with the Logan children. His is far-reaching view from atop the treehouse is a vision of inclusiveness, in which the geographical as well as social boundaries cease to separate white and black friends. Stacey's insistence that Jeremy cannot possibly see to the Logans' land is a product of the harsh life lessons he has learned throughout this book and of his growing understanding of the longstanding racial inequality in the South.

Summary and Analysis of Chapters 11-12

Chapter Eleven Summary:

The chapter begins with the words of a song beginning "Roll of thunder/hear my cry" which Mr. Morrison sings at the thunder, as he waits outside the house as he has done every night since Papa was injured. Cassie, who can't sleep, hears a tapping at the door. It is TJ. They go in the boys' room and wake up Stacey.

TJ is bruised all over his stomach and chest and thinks "something's busted" inside. His father has threatened to kick him out if he stays out another night, and he needs Stacey to help him walk home. Stacey demands an explanation, and TJ says that when he got to Strawberry with the RW and Melvin, the store was closed. They said it would be all right to take the gun and just say to anyone who saw them that they were planning to pay the next day. They send TJ, who is skinny, in through a narrow window, and then come in wearing stockings over their faces. While they are trying to break the wall cabinet with an axe, Mr. Barnett comes down to investigate and struggles with Melvin, until RW hits him over the head with the flat side of the axe.

Mrs. Barnett comes down, sees her husband slumped on the floor, and screams: "You niggers done killed Jim Lee!" She struggles with RW until she hits her head on the stove and falls to the floor. TJ is not sure if they are dead. When the Simmses won't take him straight home, TJ threatens to tell someone that they hurt the Barnetts. RW and Melvin beat him up, leave him in the back of the truck, and go to the pool hall. TJ hitches a ride past Soldier's Bridge, in order to avoid the Simmses coming home on Jackson Road, then walked to the Logans house.

Stacey wants him to stay and get Big Ma to fix his injuries but TJ insists that he has to go home. Finally, Stacey agrees to walk him home. Cassie insists on following, and then Little Man and Christopher-John wake up and decide to come too. They walk to the Avery house and watch TJ slip in through a window. Suddenly, they see lights approaching and quickly hide in the woods.

Kaleb and Thurston Wallace and RW and Melvin Simms smash their way into the Avery house and violently drag out its inhabitants. They break TJ's jaw when he emerges. One man holds up the gun, saying that RW and Melvin saw TJ and two other boys running form the Barnett's store and demanding the money they took. Kaleb kicks TJ in the stomach, knocking him down, and throws Mrs. Avery back against the house when she protests. Mr. Jamison arrives in his car and tells them to take TJ to the sheriff. The sheriff arrives and says that Mr. Granger doesn't want a hanging on his place. Kaleb Wallace wants to take TJ elsewhere to hang him and mentions hanging Mr. Morrison, too. Someone else suggests Mr. Logan. There are cries for hangings as Mr. Jamison tries to shield TJ with his own body.

Stacey insists that Cassie go tell Papa. He needs to stay in case they take TJ into the woods. Cassie and her younger brothers go to get Papa and Mr. Morrison as thunder crashes and lightening splits the sky.

Analysis:

The metaphor of thunder, which has continued throughout the book, takes center stage in this chapter, which is the crisis of the book. In the song which Mr. Morrison sings at the opening of the chapter, the reader sees the origin of the title. The full lyrics are:

Roll of thunder

hear my cry

Over the water

bye and bye

Ole man comin'

down the line

Whip in hand to

beat me down

But I ain't

gonna let him

Turn me 'round

The song is a spiritual previously sung by slaves and its presence in this chapter speaks to the continued attempts at the whites to dominate blacks seventy years after the Civil War. But the end of the song is most significant, because it portrays blacks' refusal to be dominated.

This chapter begins with "approaching thunder." Immediately after Cassie hears it, she hears TJ tapping at the door. Both sounds are marks of the approaching crisis and destruction. By the end of the chapter, a mob is clamoring to hang TJ (as well as Mr. Morrison and Papa), and the crisis is underway and inescapable.

The destruction of TJ's home and the brutal treatment of his family echoes Mr. Morrison's Christmas story about the night that his entire family was killed by a lynch mob. Earlier, TJ's refuge in the Logan house paralleled the young men who had sought safety in the Morrison home. Just as those boys unwittingly led the mob to attack the Morrisons, as the mob screams for Mr. Morrison and Papa, it seems that the accusations against TJ may lead to still more violence.

Chapter Twelve Summary:

By the time Cassie, Christopher-John, and Little Man arrive home, the adults have awakened and realized they're gone. Cassie tells TJ's story, and Papa sets off with his shotgun to stop the mob from killing TJ or finding Stacey. Mama worries that her husband will be hanged if he uses his gun and wants Mr. Granger to stop them. Papa says Granger would have already if he wanted to and leaves, telling Mama he will do what he has to do, and so will she. He and Mr. Morrison set off together in the direction of the Averys' house.

The children sit up and wait with Mama and Big Ma. Suddenly, they smell smoke. The cotton is on fire and must have been struck by lightening. If it reaches the trees, it will burn all the way to Strawberry. Mama and Big Ma set out with wet burlap and shovel sacks to fight the fire and make the children promise to remain in the house. When the boys realize that the fire is heading for the trees where Papa, Mr. Morrison, and Stacey are, they burst into tears.

Near dawn, Jeremy Simms arrives at the Logan house. He was sleeping in his treehouse, smelled the smoke, and got his father. Mr. Simms, RW, and Melvin, and the group of men from town have been all fighting the fire. Jeremy assumes that the lightening must have struck the Logans' fence post and sparked the cotton. Papa, Mr. Granger, and Stacey are all out there digging a trench together to prevent the fire from spreading. Jeremy says that the one thing that would help would be if the rain would come. He is just setting off down the road to go home when it does begin to rain. The children jump around laughing from relief in the rain.

After dawn, the fire is out after an hour of heavy rain. Cassie and Little Man head off to see what has happened, but Christopher-John won't come because they were told to stay in the house. When they get to the scene of the fire, they see that the trench was successful. Men and women covered in hats and handkerchiefs, nearly indistinguishable, continue to put out small blazes. Mr. Lanier, Mr. Simms, Mr. Granger, Papa, Mama, and Mr. Morrison all work side by side. Kaleb Wallace checks the burned stalks of cotton and does not even notice that Cassie and Little Man are staring at him.

The children rush to Mama, Big Ma, and Stacey, who tell them that Papa, Mr. Morrison, and Claude are all right but say nothing about TJ. Finally, Mama says that the sheriff and Mr. Jamison took him into Strawberry. Stacey says that the men stopped hurting TJ when Mr. Granger sent them to fight the fire, so Papa and Mr. Morrison didn't have to use guns to fight the men. The fire started, and Mr. Morrison got Stacey out of the woods. He says that Papa couldn't climb the slope with his bad leg, but Cassie is suspicious. She has seen her father move fast on that leg when he had to. Mama also assures Cassie that the taxes will get paid, despite the fact that a quarter of their cotton was burned and destroyed. She sends the three younger children in to bed, but Cassie reemerges to join Stacey on the porch.

Stacey tells her what happened after she left. The men stuffed TJ in a car, but Mr. Jamison jumped in his car and parked it across the road so that nobody could pass. Mr. Granger would not do anything more than to tell Hank Wade, the sheriff, to take care of the situation. Kaleb Wallace tried to grab Mr. Jamison's keys, which he threw into a flowerbed, and then RW and Melvin moved Mr. Jamison's car to the side of the road. Suddenly, Mr. Granger noticed smoke coming from his land and demanded that they men give TJ to the sheriff and join him in fighting the fire.

As Papa and Mr. Morrison walk up the driveway, Mr. Jamison's car pulls up. He tells them that Jim Lee Barnett died at four o'clock in the morning. TJ has a couple of broken ribs and a broken jaw but will "be all right...for now." Mr. Jamison is going to bring the Averys to town and Papa wants to go, but Mr. Morrison suggests he stay clear of the situation to avoid suspicion. Cassie is confused by this comment, until she realizes that Papa started the fire himself to keep TJ and Stacey safe. She knows that this fact is "something never to be spoken, not even to each other."

Stacey asks Papa what is going to happen to TJ and Papa says that he is in jail and could possibly go on the chain gang. Stacey asks if TJ could die and Papa says that he never lies to his son but wishes that he could now. Stacey's eyes fill with tears and he runs off into the woods. Mama and Papa tuck Cassie into bed. Only after she watches Papa setting off into the forest after Stacey does she begin to cry.

Cassie realizes that TJ will never be free to do all of the things she and her brothers do. She never liked him but he had always been there. She cries for the things which had happened that night: "for TJ. For TJ and the land."

Analysis:

When Cassie tells Papa that there is a mob clamoring to hang TJ, he says to his wife: "This thing's been coming a long time, baby, and TJ just happened to be the one foolish enough to trigger it off." A tone of inevitability pervades this chapter. All of the events of the book--the rising racial tensions, the previous incidents of violence--have led to this point. TJ is simply foolish, not evil, and only functions as a catalyst for an incident bound to happen in such a tense and violent climate.

Here, the weather metaphor of the previous chapter becomes full-fledged. The weather functions as a force as strong as that of hatred or love. It appears to be a sympathetic force, beginning to rain just when the fire cannot be stopped any other way.

In the image of men and women, black and white, working together to stop the fire, the author displays her most powerful suggestion yet of the possibility of racial harmony and cooperation. Race is symbolically erased by the bandanas and hats the people wear to protect themselves and their faces from the fire. This image suggests that, in a time of crisis, great divisions can be overcome.

However, it is important to remember that the reason that everyone fights the fire together proceeded not from an unselfish impulse but from Mr. Granger's desire to protect his own land. Here and throughout the book, Mr. Granger is a foil for Papa. The men have many surprising similarities, and both place an enormous importance on land and on family. While these feelings spur Papa to protect others, they lead Mr. Granger to act selfishly, hurting or ignoring others. Because of these parallels, however, Papa is able to conceive of a way to make Mr. Granger act by appealing to what he holds dear: his land rather than his sense of justice.

The book has a dual focus on the earth and on human life. Cassie's thoughts conclude the book, and she realizes that some things like the mud and the dust will pass away, while others, like her memory of this night will not. She cries for TJ and the land, for both have been punished for things beyond their control.

Suggested Essay Questions

1. What is the effect created by the author telling this story from the perspective of a child? Does it make the racial incidents seem more or less sinister?
2. Analyze the non-corrupt white characters like Jeremy Simms. Can you identify any others? What seems to motivate them? Are they better or worse off than the black characters?
3. Analyze the effect of the three different time periods that have to do with this novel on the text. Discuss how slavery times (before the book was set), Jim Crow laws (during when the book was set), and the Black Power movement (after the book was set, when Mildred Taylor was writing it) have influenced the text. Where do you find examples of each?
4. Discuss the role of nature in this novel. Does it work in opposition to human interests?
5. Analyze Big Mama as the voice of history. What sorts of stories does she tell, and what type of effect does she hope that these stories will have on her grandchildren's lives?
6. Roll of Thunder, Hear my Cry is as much a coming of age story for Stacey as it is for Cassie. What realities must Stacey face in this novel and what positive or negative qualities does he begin to demonstrate?
7. Describe the way that Christmas is portrayed in this novel. Does it introduce new themes relating to family life or enlarge on old ones?
8. Analyze the character of TJ. Does the author intend him to represent a typical black young man? What is his tragic flaw?
9. Compare the friendship that Stacey has with TJ to the friendship that he has with Jeremy Simms. To whom does he show more loyalty? Why?
10. When Papa sets fire to his own cotton at the end of the novel, is he acting in a defeated or a self-controlled manner? Is this a moment of triumph or of despair? Of optimism or pessimism?

Mildred Taylor and the Black Power Movement

Published in 1976, Roll of Thunder, Hear My Cry is a product not only of the Civil Rights Era but also of the Black Power Era. In 1966, James Meredith, the first black student to attend the University of Mississippi, was shot and killed by a sniper during a civil rights march. This incident, of which Taylor was well aware, led Stokely Carmichael, H. Rap Brown, and other members of the Student Nonviolent Coordinating Committee to begin a campaign for Black Power. They sought to put increased political and economic control in black hands who were independent of whites altogether. Upon returning to the United States from Africa, Taylor joined the Black Student Alliance at the University of Colorado and worked toward these aims.

As an outgrowth of the Black Power Movement, black students began to seek increased academic attention to the historical, scholarly, and cultural contributions of black Americans, many of whom had been left out of traditional histories and curricula. Taylor was a member of the Black Education Program at the University of Colorado, which, along with similar organizations at other colleges, began to push for universities to form African-American Studies departments for the interdisciplinary study of black history, culture, and scholarship. This discipline has since become a staple of many liberal arts colleges.

Based on stories about her own family members and set in a realistic historical context, Roll of Thunder, Hear My Cry is Taylor's own alternative history, a rewriting that undoes the exclusion of blacks from the national consciousness. In her novel, the effects of the Depression are not limited to white Southern farmers as they are in many history books, but are keenly felt by blacks both economically and in the form of increased racial tensions. The fact that Taylor wrote her painful and sometimes violent story for children rather than adults demonstrates the significance of these stories as part of American history, and her intention that they be taught in the elementary and middle school classroom. The widespread popularity and acceptance of Taylor's book, which continues to hold a place on many school reading lists, shows how attitudes toward inclusionary history had begun to change by the mid-seventies.

Author of ClassicNote and Sources

Carrie-Anne Dedeo, author of ClassicNote. Completed on August 13, 2000, copyright held by GradeSaver.

Updated and revised Rachel Nolan June 20, 2006. Copyright held by GradeSaver.

Linda K. Christian-Smith. The Politics of the Textbook. New York: Routledge, 1991.

Mildred Taylor. The Land. New York: Phyllis Fogelman Books, 2001.

Taylor, Mildred. Roll of Thunder, Hear My Cry 1976.

Quiz 1

1. **Mildred Taylor dedicates her book to**
   A. her daughter, for whom the book is a family history
   B. her father, on whom she based David and Stacey
   C. her grandmother, the real Big Ma
   D. her mother, who was the inspiration for Cassie

2. **How old is Cassie?**
   A. 9
   B. 10
   C. 11
   D. 12

3. **What month do the Logan children start school?**
   A. August
   B. October
   C. November
   D. September

4. **The Logan property is divided from the Granger property by what?**
   A. a stream
   B. a large boulder
   C. an oak tree
   D. a dirt road

5. **How many acres of land do the Logans own?**
   A. 20
   B. 40
   C. 200
   D. 400

6. **Where does Papa work when he is away from home?**
   A. on the railroad in Lousiana
   B. in a coal mine in Memphis
   C. as a farm hand in the Delta
   D. in a steel mill in Pennsylvania

7. **What grade does Mama teach?**
   A. seventh
   B. fifth
   C. tenth
   D. first

8. **Students from which three plantations attend Great Faith Elementary?**
   A. Wallace, Harrison, and Lanier
   B. Granger, Harrison, and Barnett
   C. Granger, Montier, and Harrison
   D. Simms, Wallace, and Jamison

9. **When Little Man reads the inside cover of his book, what does he do?**
   A. throws it at the teacher and starts to cry
   B. tosses it in the trash can and runs out of the room
   C. knocks it off his desk and ignores it
   D. flings it on the floor and stomps on it

10. **What accusation led to the Berry's burning?**
   A. John Henry was accused of stealing a watermelon
   B. Samuel was accused of injuring a white man in a fight
   C. Beacon was accused of stealing from the Barnett Mercantile
   D. John Henry was accused of flirting with a white woman

11. **When the school bus passes them on the road in the rain, the Logan children**
   A. wade through puddles
   B. jump to the muddy banks
   C. fall into the gully
   D. run into the forest

12. **Immediately after the incident with the bus, Stacey asks his siblings to**
   A. go with him to the Wallace store
   B. go to the toolshed at lunchtime
   C. meet him at the crossroads after school
   D. wait behind the school the next morning

13. **After the bus gets stuck in the ditch, the driver**
   A. tries to repair the motor with the help of the Wallaces
   B. sends the students home and leaves the bus until the rain stops
   C. catches the Logan children in the woods
   D. has his passengers push it out of the mud

14. **The night men whom Cassie watches pass the Logan house in their cars are after**
   A. Sam Tatum for calling Mr. Barnett a liar
   B. Cassie and Stacey for breaking the bus
   C. TJ for stealing a gun
   D. Beacon Berry for molesting a white woman

15. **What book does Stacey catch TJ holding in Mama's room?**
   A. Booker T. Washington's Up from Slavery
   B. Frederick Douglass's Narrative of the Life of Frederick Douglass
   C. Harriet Beecher Stowe's Uncle Tom's Cabin
   D. WEB DuBois's The Negro

16. **How was the glade in the forest on the Logans' land made?**
   A. by lumbermen who cut trees down illegally
   B. by the natural beach around the pond
   C. by logs that Grandpa cut down to build the Logan farmhouse
   D. by a fire set by Papa

17. **When Big Ma met Paul Edward, what was he doing?**
   A. working on the railroad in Memphis
   B. working in a furniture store in Vicksburg
   C. tenant-farming land in the Delta
   D. hiding from his former masters in Strawberry

18. **When did Paul Edward buy the first Logan-owned land?**
   A. 1865
   B. 1887
   C. 1910
   D. 1918

19. **At Barnett's Mercantile in Strawberry, what does TJ admire?**
   A. a Packard
   B. a pearl-handled pistol
   C. a pearl necklace
   D. a shotgun

20. **What leads Mr. Barnett to throw Cassie out of his store?**
   A. She reminds him to wait on TJ
   B. He only serves whites in his store
   C. She accuses him of lying
   D. He accuses her of stealing

21. **What does Lillian Jean do when Cassie bumps into her?**
   A. Fakes tears and calls for her father
   B. Falls off the sidewalk and demands an apology
   C. Threatens to get the night men after her
   D. Tells her to get off the sidewalk and pushes her

22. **When Cassie tells him about the incident in Strawberry, what does Uncle Hammer do?**
   A. Heeds Mama's pleas and stays in the house all night
   B. Threatens Charlie Simms with his gun
   C. Tells Cassie that sometimes its safer to do what white folks say
   D. Drives around talking with Mr. Morrison

23. **What does Cassie notice about Mama's shoes as she gets ready for church?**
   A. They are heirlooms that used to belong to her own mother
   B. She is wearing a shiny new pair given to her by Uncle Hammer
   C. There are holes in the soles patched with cardboard
   D. They are actually a pair of Papa's old shoes, stuffed with newspaper

24. **What story does Cassie know about the name of Soldiers Road?**
   A. Rebel soldiers had marched up the road to protect Strawberry
   B. Rebel soldiers had surrendered on that road after a long battle
   C. Runaway slaves had used the road when joining the Northern army
   D. Yankee soldiers had marched down the road when attacking the town

25. **When Mama finds out that Stacey gave TJ his coat, what does she want him to do?**
    A. Get the coat back when he has grown into it
    B. Leave the coat with TJ permanently
    C. Bring back the coat immediately
    D. Pay Uncle Hammer back for the coat

Quiz 1 Answer Key

1. **(B)** her father, on whom she based David and Stacey
2. **(A)** 9
3. **(B)** October
4. **(C)** an oak tree
5. **(D)** 400
6. **(A)** on the railroad in Lousiana
7. **(A)** seventh
8. **(C)** Granger, Montier, and Harrison
9. **(D)** flings it on the floor and stomps on it
10. **(D)** John Henry was accused of flirting with a white woman
11. **(C)** fall into the gully
12. **(B)** go to the toolshed at lunchtime
13. **(B)** sends the students home and leaves the bus until the rain stops
14. **(A)** Sam Tatum for calling Mr. Barnett a liar
15. **(D)** WEB DuBois's The Negro
16. **(A)** by lumbermen who cut trees down illegally
17. **(B)** working in a furniture store in Vicksburg
18. **(B)** 1887
19. **(B)** a pearl-handled pistol
20. **(A)** She reminds him to wait on TJ
21. **(D)** Tells her to get off the sidewalk and pushes her
22. **(D)** Drives around talking with Mr. Morrison
23. **(C)** There are holes in the soles patched with cardboard
24. **(A)** Rebel soldiers had marched up the road to protect Strawberry
25. **(C)** Bring back the coat immediately

Quiz 2

1. **What does Mr. Morrison say about the Christmas that he was six and his family died?**
   A. He remembers the story because it's been told to him many times
   B. He was too young to remember anything
   C. He remembers it because he makes himself remember it
   D. He tries not to think about it but it comes back in nightmares

2. **Who agrees to back the credit of the families shopping in Vicksburg?**
   A. Mr. Granger
   B. Mr. Jamison
   C. Papa
   D. Uncle Hammer

3. **Cassie makes sure that Lillian Jean won't tell on her for beating her up because**
   A. Cassie threatens to beat her up again if she does
   B. Cassie will tell the secrets Lillian Jean has shared about her friends
   C. Jeremy has promised to keep her from telling
   D. She would be embarrassed to be beaten up by a black girl

4. **What is Mama teaching about when the representatives of the school board visit her classroom?**
   A. The history of slavery and its economic effects
   B. Black literature in the form of slave narratives of the nineteenth century
   C. Black gospel music and its Biblical origins
   D. The geography of Africa and the origins of the slaves

5. **When Stacey shuns him, TJ begins hanging around with**
   A. Little Willie Wiggins and Moe Turner
   B. Jeremy and Charlie Simms
   C. RW and Melvin Simms
   D. Kaleb and Dewberry Wallace

6. **Why does Papa compare the Logans to a fig tree?**
   A. "We may be small but we're darn strong."
   B. "We can produce whatever we need, every year without fail."
   C. "We're part of the earth and the earth's part of us."
   D. "We keep doing what we gotta do, and we don't give up."

7. **On the way back from Vicksburg, what happens to Papa?**
   A. He is tarred and feathered by the Wallaces
   B. He is shot at by the Wallaces and has his leg broken when the wagon rolls over it
   C. He is beaten by the Wallaces, who threaten to have him hanged
   D. He falls off the wagon and breaks his leg when the Wallaces ram it with their truck

8. **How do the Logans manage to pay the bank note?**
   A. Uncle Hammer sells his car and gives the family the money
   B. They borrow the money from Mr. Jamison
   C. They sell some of their land to Mr. Granger
   D. Papa cuts down and sells the trees

9. **When and for how long is the annual revival?**
   A. For three days, beginning the first of June
   B. July fourth, for one day
   C. The first two weeks of October
   D. Beginning the third Sunday of August, for seven days

10. **Where does the title Roll of Thunder, Hear My Cry come from?**
   A. A poem Cassie writes for school
   B. A song Mr. Morrison sings at the approaching thunder
   C. A hymn sung in church during the revival
   D. A prayer Big Ma recites in times of stress

11. **Why does TJ say he has to get home in the middle of the night?**
   A. He's scared and knows his family will know how to help him
   B. His mother is the only one who can fix his injuries
   C. His father threatened to kick him out of the house if he stayed out all night again
   D. His new "friends" are looking for him and he needs to hide

12. **What happened to Mr. Barnett during the break-in?**
   A. TJ pushed him and he hit his head against the stove
   B. Melvin stabbed him with a pocket knife
   C. Melvin shot him with the pearl handled pistol
   D. RW hit him over the head with an axe

13. **Who is the sole man to directly confront and argue with the lynch mob at the Avery house?**
    A. The sheriff, who demands that they give him custody of TJ
    B. Papa, who threatens them with his shotgun
    C. Mr. Granger, who orders them off his land
    D. Mr. Jamison, who tells them to hand TJ over to the sheriff

14. **What started and what stops the fire?**
    A. Mr. Morrison and a counter-fire
    B. Papa and the rain
    C. Lightening and a trench
    D. A dropped lantern and a bucket brigade

15. **Who finally stops the mob from hanging TJ, and what ultimately happens to TJ?**

    A. Mr. Granger, by sending the mob to fight the fire and save his land, stops the mob. TJ will be put on a chain gang.

    B. Mr. Jamison, by blocking the road with his car, stops the mob. TJ is returned to his parents.

    C. Mr. Granger, seeking to protect his land from violence, stops the mob. After a trial, TJ will be hung.

    D. The sheriff, by sending the mob to fight the fire, stops the mob. TJ is arrested and will be sent to prison.

16. **Who is the least adventurous Logan?**
    A. Cassie
    B. Stacey
    C. Christopher-John
    D. Papa

17. **Who is the cleanest Logan child?**
    A. Cassie
    B. Stacey
    C. Little Man
    D. Christopher-John

18. **Who is wearing a new dress on the first day of school?**
    A. Cassie
    B. Mary-Lou
    C. Mama
    D. Lillian Jean

19. **In addition to being a store, the Wallace's place functions as a**

A. swimming pool
B. dance hall
C. courtroom
D. farm

20. **Where does Cassie have to sit at school?**

A. outside
B. in the back
C. next to Mama
D. in the front

21. **Who is the eldest?**

A. Stacey
B. RW Simms
C. TJ
D. Casey

22. **Why does Mrs. Barnett think that the Simmses are black?**

A. they wear stocking caps over their faces
B. they are black
C. they paint their faces
D. because they are with TJ

23. **What do the youngest boys get for Christmas?**

A. cars
B. scholarships to college
C. books
D. shoes

24. **What does Granger say that Mama can do now that he has fired her?**

A. sell him her land
B. move to Vicksburg
C. write her own book
D. raise her family properly

25. **How many men fire Mama?**

A. one
B. two
C. none
D. three

Quiz 2 Answer Key

1. **(C)** He remembers it because he makes himself remember it
2. **(B)** Mr. Jamison
3. **(B)** Cassie will tell the secrets Lillian Jean has shared about her friends
4. **(A)** The history of slavery and its economic effects
5. **(C)** RW and Melvin Simms
6. **(D)** "We keep doing what we gotta do, and we don't give up."
7. **(B)** He is shot at by the Wallaces and has his leg broken when the wagon rolls over it
8. **(A)** Uncle Hammer sells his car and gives the family the money
9. **(D)** Beginning the third Sunday of August, for seven days
10. **(B)** A song Mr. Morrison sings at the approaching thunder
11. **(C)** His father threatened to kick him out of the house if he stayed out all night again
12. **(D)** RW hit him over the head with an axe
13. **(D)** Mr. Jamison, who tells them to hand TJ over to the sheriff
14. **(B)** Papa and the rain
15. **(A)** Mr. Granger, by sending the mob to fight the fire and save his land, stops the mob. TJ will be put on a chain gang.
16. **(C)** Christopher-John
17. **(C)** Little Man
18. **(B)** Mary-Lou
19. **(B)** dance hall
20. **(D)** in the front
21. **(B)** RW Simms
22. **(A)** they wear stocking caps over their faces
23. **(C)** books
24. **(C)** write her own book
25. **(D)** three

Quiz 3

1. **Where does Mama take her children when she finds out that they have been to the Wallace store?**
   A. to Strawberry
   B. to the railroad
   C. to see the Berrys
   D. to see Hammer

2. **Why was Mr. Morrison fired?**
   A. he got in a fight with some black men
   B. he got in a fight with some white men
   C. he got in a fight with his boss
   D. he slept with a white woman

3. **Why is Mr. Morrison so strong?**
   A. the railroad made him strong
   B. he has worked on construction
   C. he works out a lot
   D. his parents were bred during slavery

4. **What crop do the Logans grow?**
   A. cotton
   B. avocados
   C. cane
   D. strawberry

5. **How long is the duration of the book?**
   A. two years
   B. five years
   C. six months
   D. a year

6. **Mildred grew up in the**
   A. Northeast
   B. West
   C. North
   D. South

7. **How does Mama find out about the inside covers of the books?**
   A. from Cassie's teacher
   B. from the school board
   C. from Little Man
   D. from Cassie

8. **Who is Stacey's only white friend?**
   A. RW Simms
   B. TJ
   C. Melvin Simms
   D. Jeremy Simms

9. **Big Mama is known for her skills in**
   A. baking
   B. healing
   C. running
   D. preaching

10. **Cassie shares a bed with**
   A. Big Mama
   B. TJ
   C. Mama
   D. Lillian Jean

11. **After Cassie sees the night men, Mama thinks that**
   A. she shouldn't be allowed to leave the house
   B. she needs to go back to school
   C. she was involved in the bus incident
   D. she is sick

12. **Stacey stops being friends with TJ when**
   A. he runs away from home
   B. he takes his coat
   C. he steals things
   D. he gets his mother fired

13. **What was Hammer's Christmas present to Stacey?**
   A. a house
   B. a new coat
   C. new shoes
   D. a car

14. **How does Hammer help to pay the bank note?**
   A. he gets married
   B. he sells his car
   C. he moves back to the farm
   D. he works on the railroad

15. **Hammer is**
   A. single
   B. married
   C. divorced
   D. a widower

16. **When the Wallaces see Hammer in his new car, they think that he is**
   A. the new mayor
   B. Harlan Granger
   C. Mr. Jamison
   D. Mr. Montier

17. **Mama whips Stacey for**
   A. writing cheat notes
   B. having TJ's cheat notes
   C. looking through her test materials at home
   D. talking with TJ during the test

18. **Sharecroppers**
   A. are the same as slaves
   B. pay rent
   C. pay a portion of their crops instead of rent
   D. own their own land

19. **The weather acts as a force**

A. representing despair
B. sympathetic to humans
C. seperate from human life
D. representing injustice

20. **Mr. Turner agrees to participate in the boycott if**

A. if the Logans pay for his groceries
B. if he can come with them to Vicksburg
C. someone will back his signature
D. if he can live on their farm

21. **The person that agrees to back the sharecroppers' signatures is**

A. Mr. Berry
B. Mr. Granger
C. Mr. Jamison
D. Mr. Morrison

22. **Mr. Jamison's office is**

A. in town
B. in Strawberry
C. at his farm
D. in Vicksburg

23. **The Logans drive a**

A. carriage
B. car
C. automobile
D. railroad car

24. **At the beginning of the novel, Papa is away at**

A. the law office
B. Hammer's office
C. the railroad
D. another farm

25. **TJ says that he wants the pistol**

A. to fish

B. to hunt

C. to murder the Simmses

D. to protect himself

Quiz 3 Answer Key

1. **(C)** to see the Berrys
2. **(B)** he got in a fight with some white men
3. **(D)** his parents were bred during slavery
4. **(A)** cotton
5. **(D)** a year
6. **(C)** North
7. **(A)** from Cassie's teacher
8. **(D)** Jeremy Simms
9. **(B)** healing
10. **(A)** Big Mama
11. **(D)** she is sick
12. **(D)** he gets his mother fired
13. **(D)** a car
14. **(B)** he sells his car
15. **(A)** single
16. **(B)** Harlan Granger
17. **(B)** having TJ's cheat notes
18. **(C)** pay a portion of their crops instead of rent
19. **(B)** sympathetic to humans
20. **(C)** someone will back his signature
21. **(C)** Mr. Jamison
22. **(B)** in Strawberry
23. **(A)** carriage
24. **(C)** the railroad
25. **(D)** to protect himself

Quiz 4

1. **How does Mr. Simms force Cassie to apologize to his daughter?**
   A. by asking her nicely
   B. by twisting her arm behind her back
   C. by slapping her
   D. by threatening to take her land

2. **Who prevents Hammer from acting violently towards the Simmses?**
   A. Stacey
   B. TJ
   C. Papa
   D. Mr. Morrison

3. **The Logans' mule is named**
   A. Jim
   B. Jack
   C. Paul
   D. Simon

4. **Soldier's Bridge was built**
   A. quite recently
   B. before the American Revolution
   C. before the Civil War
   D. during the Civil War

5. **Hammer, when he finds out that Stacey has temporarily given away the coat, insists that he**
   A. get it back from TJ
   B. join the chain gang
   C. go to school with no shoes
   D. let TJ keep it

6. **Most children that Cassie knows have no**
   A. clothing
   B. education
   C. shoes
   D. money

7. **The name for a mob of white men in this novel is usually**
   A. the klu klux klan
   B. the riders
   C. the night men
   D. the white men

8. **Mr. Morrison's family was killed in**
   A. a flood
   B. an attack by white people
   C. a fire
   D. the Civil War

9. **Granger argues that he will get the land back easily from the Logans because**
   A. they are in debt
   B. they are stupid
   C. of their boycott
   D. they are unpopular

10. **Big Mama signs the deed for the land over to**
   A. Cassie
   B. Hammer
   C. Papa
   D. her two sons

11. **TJ's little brother is named**
   A. Melvin
   B. Jeremy
   C. RW
   D. Claude

12. **Jeremy sleeps in**
   A. his house
   B. Stacey's bed
   C. a treehouse
   D. a tent

13. **For Christmas, Jeremy gives Stacey**
   A. a jacket
   B. some food
   C. a whistle
   D. his old shoes

14. **For Christmas, Stacey gives Jeremy**
   A. nothing
   B. a whistle
   C. a book
   D. his old shoes

15. **Cassie's Christmas present is a book by**
   A. W.E.B. DuBois
   B. Alexander Dumas
   C. Mark Twain
   D. Booker T. Washington

16. **Little Man's Christmas book is**
   A. Aesop's Fables
   B. The Three Muskateers
   C. Grimm Brothers' Maerchen
   D. The Count of Monte Cristo

17. **Big Mama is**
   A. Cassie's mother
   B. Stacey's mother
   C. Mama's mother
   D. Papa's mother

18. **Stacey feels responsible for**
   A. Cassie getting drunk
   B. Mama getting fired
   C. his Papa's leg being broken
   D. TJ getting on the chain gang

19. **Who walks three and a half hours to school?**
    A. Moe Turner
    B. the Logans
    C. Lillian Jean
    D. Jeremy Simms

20. **The Logans are**
    A. Jewish
    B. Muslim
    C. Buddhist
    D. Christian

21. **What does Mr. Morrison search the Wallaces' wagon for before he lifts it?**
    A. a package
    B. Papa
    C. a gun
    D. a body

22. **What day does TJ steal the pistol on?**
    A. the day of the revival
    B. his mother's birthday
    C. Christmas
    D. his birthday

23. **After beating the Barnetts, the Simmses**
    A. confess to the police
    B. rob a bank
    C. smoke a cigarette
    D. beat TJ

24. **The title comes from**
    A. another novel
    B. a historical treatise
    C. a spiritual song
    D. a poem

25. **The Simmses kill**

A. Mr. Barnett
B. the Berrys
C. the whole Barnett family
D. the Wallaces

Quiz 4 Answer Key

1. **(B)** by twisting her arm behind her back
2. **(D)** Mr. Morrison
3. **(B)** Jack
4. **(C)** before the Civil War
5. **(D)** let TJ keep it
6. **(C)** shoes
7. **(C)** the night men
8. **(B)** an attack by white people
9. **(C)** of their boycott
10. **(D)** her two sons
11. **(D)** Claude
12. **(C)** a treehouse
13. **(C)** a whistle
14. **(A)** nothing
15. **(B)** Alexander Dumas
16. **(A)** Aesop's Fables
17. **(D)** Papa's mother
18. **(C)** his Papa's leg being broken
19. **(A)** Moe Turner
20. **(D)** Christian
21. **(C)** a gun
22. **(A)** the day of the revival
23. **(D)** beat TJ
24. **(C)** a spiritual song
25. **(A)** Mr. Barnett

ClassicNotes

Getting you the grade since 1999™

Other ClassicNotes from GradeSaver™

1984
Absalom, Absalom
Adam Bede
The Adventures of Augie March
The Adventures of Huckleberry Finn
The Adventures of Tom Sawyer
The Aeneid
Agamemnon
The Age of Innocence
The Alchemist (Coelho)
The Alchemist (Jonson)
Alice in Wonderland
All My Sons
All Quiet on the Western Front
All the King's Men
All the Pretty Horses
Allen Ginsberg's Poetry
The Ambassadors
American Beauty
And Then There Were None
Angela's Ashes
Animal Farm
Anna Karenina
Anthem
Antigone
Antony and Cleopatra
Aristotle's Ethics
Aristotle's Poetics
Aristotle's Politics
As I Lay Dying
As You Like It
Astrophil and Stella
Atlas Shrugged
Atonement
The Awakening
Babbitt
The Bacchae
Bartleby the Scrivener
The Bean Trees
The Bell Jar
Beloved
Benito Cereno
Beowulf
Bhagavad-Gita
Billy Budd
Black Boy
Bleak House
Bless Me, Ultima
Blindness
Blood Wedding
The Bloody Chamber
Bluest Eye
The Bonfire of the Vanities
The Book of the Duchess and Other Poems
The Book Thief
Brave New World
Breakfast at Tiffany's
Breakfast of Champions
The Brief Wondrous Life of Oscar Wao
The Brothers Karamazov
The Burning Plain and Other Stories
A Burnt-Out Case
By Night in Chile
Call of the Wild
Candide
The Canterbury Tales
Cat on a Hot Tin Roof
Cat's Cradle
Catch-22
The Catcher in the Rye
The Caucasian Chalk Circle
Charlotte Temple
Charlotte's Web
The Cherry Orchard
The Chocolate War
The Chosen
A Christmas Carol
Christopher Marlowe's Poems
Chronicle of a Death Foretold
Civil Disobedience
Civilization and Its Discontents
A Clockwork Orange
Coleridge's Poems
The Color of Water
The Color Purple
Comedy of Errors
Communist Manifesto
A Confederacy of Dunces
Confessions
Connecticut Yankee in King Arthur's Court
The Consolation of Philosophy
Coriolanus

For our full list of over 250 Study Guides, Quizzes, Sample College Application Essays, Literature Essays and E-texts, visit:

www.gradesaver.com

ClassicNotes

GradeSaver™

Getting you the grade since 1999™

Other ClassicNotes from GradeSaver™

The Count of Monte Cristo
The Country Wife
Crime and Punishment
The Crucible
Cry, the Beloved Country
The Crying of Lot 49
The Curious Incident of the Dog in the Night-time
Cymbeline
Daisy Miller
David Copperfield
Death in Venice
Death of a Salesman
The Death of Ivan Ilych
Democracy in America
Devil in a Blue Dress
Dharma Bums
The Diary of a Young Girl by Anne Frank
Disgrace
Divine Comedy-I: Inferno
Do Androids Dream of Electric Sheep?
Doctor Faustus (Marlowe)
A Doll's House
Don Quixote Book I
Don Quixote Book II
Dora: An Analysis of a Case of Hysteria
Dr. Jekyll and Mr. Hyde
Dracula
Dubliners
East of Eden
Electra by Sophocles
The Electric Kool-Aid Acid Test
Emily Dickinson's Collected Poems
Emma
Ender's Game
Endgame
The English Patient
The Epic of Gilgamesh
Ethan Frome
The Eumenides
Everyman: Morality Play
Everything is Illuminated
The Faerie Queene
Fahrenheit 451
The Fall of the House of Usher
A Farewell to Arms
The Federalist Papers
Fences
Flags of Our Fathers
Flannery O'Connor's Stories
For Whom the Bell Tolls
The Fountainhead
Frankenstein
Franny and Zooey
The Giver
The Glass Castle
The Glass Menagerie
The God of Small Things
Goethe's Faust
The Good Earth
The Good Woman of Setzuan
The Grapes of Wrath
Great Expectations
The Great Gatsby
Grendel
The Guest
Gulliver's Travels
Hamlet
The Handmaid's Tale
Hard Times
Haroun and the Sea of Stories
Harry Potter and the Philosopher's Stone
Heart of Darkness
Hedda Gabler
Henry IV (Pirandello)
Henry IV Part 1
Henry IV Part 2
Henry V
Herzog
Hippolytus
The Hobbit
Homo Faber
House of Mirth
The House of the Seven Gables
The House of the Spirits
House on Mango Street
How the Garcia Girls Lost Their Accents
Howards End
A Hunger Artist
I Know Why the Caged Bird Sings

For our full list of over 250 Study Guides, Quizzes, Sample College Application Essays, Literature Essays and E-texts, visit:

www.gradesaver.com

ClassicNotes

Getting you the grade since 1999™

Other ClassicNotes from GradeSaver™

I, Claudius
An Ideal Husband
Iliad
The Importance of Being Earnest
In Cold Blood
In Our Time
In the Time of the Butterflies
Inherit the Wind
An Inspector Calls
Into the Wild
Invisible Man
The Island of Dr. Moreau
Jane Eyre
Jazz
The Jew of Malta
Joseph Andrews
The Joy Luck Club
Julius Caesar
The Jungle
Jungle of Cities
Kama Sutra
Kate Chopin's Short Stories
Kidnapped
King Lear
King Solomon's Mines
The Kite Runner
Last of the Mohicans
Leaves of Grass
The Legend of Sleepy Hollow
A Lesson Before Dying
Leviathan
Libation Bearers
Life is Beautiful
Life of Pi
Light In August
Like Water for Chocolate
The Lion, the Witch and the Wardrobe
Little Women
Lolita
Long Day's Journey Into Night
Look Back in Anger
Lord Jim
Lord of the Flies
The Lord of the Rings: The Fellowship of the Ring
The Lord of the Rings: The Return of the King
The Lord of the Rings: The Two Towers
A Lost Lady
The Lottery and Other Stories
Love in the Time of Cholera
The Love Song of J. Alfred Prufrock
The Lovely Bones
Lucy
Macbeth
Madame Bovary
Maggie: A Girl of the Streets and Other Stories
Manhattan Transfer
Mankind: Medieval Morality Plays
Mansfield Park
The Marrow of Tradition
The Master and Margarita
MAUS
The Mayor of Casterbridge
Measure for Measure
Medea
Merchant of Venice
Metamorphoses
The Metamorphosis
Middlemarch
A Midsummer Night's Dream
Moby Dick
A Modest Proposal and Other Satires
Moll Flanders
Mother Courage and Her Children
Mrs. Dalloway
Much Ado About Nothing
My Antonia
Mythology
The Namesake
Native Son
Nickel and Dimed: On (Not) Getting By in America
Night
Nine Stories
No Exit

For our full list of over 250 Study Guides, Quizzes,
Sample College Application Essays, Literature Essays and E-texts, visit:

www.gradesaver.com

ClassicNotes

GradeSaver™

Getting you the grade since 1999™

Other ClassicNotes from GradeSaver™

Northanger Abbey
Notes from Underground
O Pioneers
The Odyssey
Oedipus Rex or Oedipus the King
Of Mice and Men
The Old Man and the Sea
Oliver Twist
On Liberty
On the Road
One Day in the Life of Ivan Denisovich
One Flew Over the Cuckoo's Nest
One Hundred Years of Solitude
Oroonoko
Oryx and Crake
Othello
Our Town
The Outsiders
Pale Fire
Pamela: Or Virtue Rewarded
Paradise Lost
A Passage to India
The Pearl
Percy Shelley: Poems
Perfume: The Story of a Murderer
Persepolis: The Story of a Childhood
Persuasion
Phaedra
Phaedrus
The Piano Lesson
The Picture of Dorian Gray
Poe's Poetry
Poe's Short Stories
Poems of W.B. Yeats: The Rose
Poems of W.B. Yeats: The Tower
The Poems of William Blake
The Poetry of Robert Frost
The Poisonwood Bible
Pope's Poems and Prose
Portrait of the Artist as a Young Man
Pride and Prejudice
The Prince
The Professor's House
Prometheus Bound
Pudd'nhead Wilson
Pygmalion
Rabbit, Run
A Raisin in the Sun
The Real Life of Sebastian Knight
Rebecca
The Red Badge of Courage
The Remains of the Day
The Republic
Rhinoceros
Richard II
Richard III
The Rime of the Ancient Mariner
Rip Van Winkle and Other Stories
The Road
Robinson Crusoe
Roll of Thunder, Hear My Cry
Romeo and Juliet
A Room of One's Own
A Room With a View
A Rose For Emily and Other Short Stories
Rosencrantz and Guildenstern Are Dead
Salome
The Scarlet Letter
The Scarlet Pimpernel
The Seagull
Season of Migration to the North
Second Treatise of Government
The Secret Life of Bees
The Secret River
Secret Sharer
Sense and Sensibility
A Separate Peace
Shakespeare's Sonnets
Shantaram
Short Stories of Ernest Hemingway
Short Stories of F. Scott Fitzgerald
Siddhartha

For our full list of over 250 Study Guides, Quizzes,
Sample College Application Essays, Literature Essays and E-texts, visit:

www.gradesaver.com

ClassicNotes

GradeSaver™

Getting you the grade since 1999™

Other ClassicNotes from GradeSaver™

Silas Marner
Sir Gawain and the Green Knight
Sister Carrie
Six Characters in Search of an Author
Slaughterhouse Five
Snow Falling on Cedars
The Social Contract
Something Wicked This Way Comes
Song of Roland
Song of Solomon
Songs of Innocence and of Experience
Sons and Lovers
The Sorrows of Young Werther
The Sound and the Fury
The Spanish Tragedy
Spenser's Amoretti and Epithalamion
Spring Awakening
The Stranger
A Streetcar Named Desire
Sula
The Sun Also Rises
Tale of Two Cities
The Taming of the Shrew
The Tempest
Tender is the Night
Tess of the D'Urbervilles
Their Eyes Were Watching God
Things Fall Apart
The Things They Carried
A Thousand Splendid Suns
The Threepenny Opera
Through the Looking Glass
Thus Spoke Zarathustra
The Time Machine
Titus Andronicus
To Build a Fire
To Kill a Mockingbird
To the Lighthouse
The Tortilla Curtain
Touching Spirit Bear
Treasure Island
Trifles
Troilus and Cressida
Tropic of Cancer
Tropic of Capricorn
Tuesdays With Morrie
The Turn of the Screw
Twelfth Night
Twilight
Ulysses
Uncle Tom's Cabin
Utopia
Vanity Fair
A Very Old Man With Enormous Wings
Villette
The Visit
Volpone
Waiting for Godot
Waiting for Lefty
Walden
Washington Square
The Waste Land
The Wealth of Nations
Where the Red Fern Grows
White Fang
A White Heron and Other Stories
White Noise
White Teeth
Who's Afraid of Virginia Woolf
Wide Sargasso Sea
Wieland
Winesburg, Ohio
The Winter's Tale
The Woman Warrior
Wordsworth's Poetical Works
Woyzeck
A Wrinkle in Time
Wuthering Heights
The Yellow Wallpaper
Yonnondio: From the Thirties
Zeitoun

For our full list of over 250 Study Guides, Quizzes, Sample College Application Essays, Literature Essays and E-texts, visit:

www.gradesaver.com

54067348R00060

Made in the USA
San Bernardino,
CA